FROM THE MIND TO
THE MARKETPLACE

FROM THE MIND TO THE MARKETPLACE

The Story of an Inventor,
the Home Improvement Industry,
His Wife and Her Lovers

Jayne Seagrave

Copyright © 2005 by Jayne Seagrave
First edition

Library and Archives Canada Cataloguing in Publication

Seagrave, Jayne, 1961-
    From the mind to the marketplace: the story of an inventor, the home
improvement industry, his wife and her lovers / Jayne Seagrave.

ISBN 1-894384-93-8

    1. Inventions—Marketing. 2. New products—Marketing. 3. Seagrave,
Jayne, 1961–   . 4. Dewberry, Andrew. 5. Vancouver Tool Corporation. 6.
Inventors—Canada—Biography. I. Title.

TH915.S42 2005   608'.068'8
C2005-900072-4

Cover photos courtesy of Derek Norris, Looking Good Photography. Cover
and book design and layout by Darlene Nickull. Edited by Barbara Tomlin.
Selected photos courtesy of Michael Nikolich.

Heritage House acknowledges the financial support for its publishing program
from the Government of Canada through the Book Publishing Industry
Development Program (BPIDP), Canada Council for the Arts, and the
Province of British Columbia through the British Columbia Arts Council.

Heritage House Publishing Ltd.
#108-17665 66A Ave.
Surrey, BC, Canada
V3S 2A7
greatbooks@heritagehouse.ca
www.heritagehouse.ca

Printed in Canada

The Canada Council | Le Conseil des Arts
for the Arts | du Canada

BRITISH
COLUMBIA
ARTS COUNCIL
We acknowledge the support of the Province of British Columbia
through the British Columbia Arts Council

For Len Buonassisi,
Magnet Home Hardware, Vancouver, B.C.,
who purchased the first Caulk-Rite tool in July 1996.

Contents

Acknowledgements

This book and the story it contains would not have been possible without a number of individuals in the home improvement industry who took the plunge and decided to risk purchasing a new product from a small, unknown Canadian company. For this leap of faith and for their continued support I am forever indebted to the buyers at Home Hardware, Dynamic Paint Products, Canadian Tire, RONA and Apollo Exports International. I am also indebted to our suppliers (specifically Valcraft Printing and Packaging, Aeon Pacific Manufacturing, Advance Plastics, Canplastic Manufacturing, Custom Gaskets, Hansen Industries and McLogo Design Agency), who have contributed significantly to the growth and development of Vancouver Tool.

In addition I am grateful to the individuals who commented on sections and earlier drafts of this text, including participants in the UBC Summer Writing Program in 2004, various friends and, of course, my husband, Andrew Dewberry. A number of individuals were also successful in taking the words in a rough manuscript to a professionally printed format, including Barbara Tomlin and Darlene Nickull. I am also indebted to Rodger Touchie and his excellent staff at Heritage House, who have continued to support my writing ambitions with this project as they have with others.

Finally I would like to thank my family, specifically Jack and Sam, for taking me to numerous parks and indoor entertainment establishments and leaving me to write and edit while they ran wild, and to Andrew for being the "Mad Inventor" and for not in any way restricting my enthusiasm, ambitions and dreams.

While all these individuals and companies had a direct influence on this story, at the end of the day this book is my own personal recollection and interpretation of the events that led to the birth, growth and eventual success of the Vancouver Tool Corporation.

Jayne Seagrave
December 2004

Introduction

Nine years ago my husband and I established the Vancouver Tool Corporation so that we could produce and promote a specialized tool for the application of caulking. My husband served as the inventor while I undertook all the sales and marketing tasks in an effort to place our product with retail giants such as Canadian Tire, Home Depot and Home Hardware. I did this with no background in sales and marketing. In fact, my background is in academia. I have a Ph.D. in criminology and have spent more years lecturing students and writing academic papers than I have approaching buyers and crafting press releases.

Today our company provides more than 10 different products to an array of retailers and does enough business to allow us a very comfortable life. For the last three years my husband has been president of the B.C. Inventors Society, and I have given numerous presentations to this group on marketing. The Vancouver Tool Corporation has been featured in *Reader's Digest, B.C. Business, Business in Vancouver* and *The Entrepreneur*. In 2005 we will be profiled by the American Home Based Business Association in its literature and through an infomercial.

So how did we manage all this? To begin with, we had a fortunate combination of personal qualities and abilities (especially my husband's skills as an inventor and my skills as a researcher). We also benefited from having a supportive network of friends and family and the right economic climate. But this is not to say that we didn't have problems and didn't need to learn a lot along the way. We did. This book describes how we came up with our first product (Chapter 1) and learned about prototyping and production (Chapter 2). The text goes on to describe what we found out about the home improvement industry (Chapter 3) and marketing a product (Chapter 4 and Chapter 5). Finally, this book describes what happened when we came up with other products (Chapter 6), explored new markets (Chapter 7) and then considered what to do next (Chapter 8).

You will be particularly interested in our story if you have an idea for a totally new product and you want to learn how the invention can be taken from the mind to the marketplace successfully.

CHAPTER 1: The Birth of an Invention

One Man's Hobby Becomes Serious Business

My husband Andrew and I had been in the inventing business about two years when my mother sent us an article from a magazine advising any would-be inventor to invent something "small, cheap, plastic and mass-marketable." Andrew's first invention certainly had not matched this description. In 1988 when I moved from London, England, to Manchester to live with Andrew, I brought with me all my possessions loaded in a small hatchback car. Within four days of my arrival Andrew borrowed this vehicle and returned six hours later with a huge grey soaker tub tied to the roof. This was his first invention (aside from the countless rockets and spaceships invented during childhood when he was supposed to be asleep in bed). The tub was definitely not the invention recommended by the adviser in my mother's article, and it ended up living in our basement, untouched for years. Welcome to the Inventor's World.

In 1991 we moved from England to Vancouver so that I could start my studies for a Ph.D. in criminology at Simon

Fraser University. Andrew had never been to North America before, but within three days had decided he wanted to stay. I had previously lived in Ottawa for two years and during that time had visited British Columbia. Like countless people before us, we loved B.C. We became Canadian citizens three years later.

I studied at SFU from September 1991 until March 1995. While I was studying Andrew was working as a project manager for Emily Carr College of Art and Design and then for the University of British Columbia. During the time he was not working or renovating our house, he was inventing. We did not have a vast amount of money and had managed to purchase a "fixer-upper," which we spent every weekend improving. It was while installing the second bathroom and dealing with the messy task of caulking that Andrew invented Caulk-Rite, a tool for applying caulk.

"That pathetic little plastic tool"

The Caulk-Rite tool, which one of my girlfriends once described as "that pathetic little plastic tool," is a small implement about 4½ inches long with a rubber blade at one end. Once silicon or latex caulk has been applied to a sink or bathtub the Caulk-Rite tool smoothes the caulk, compresses it into the joint, collects the excess and creates the perfect caulking bead. While there are other caulking tools on the market, none work as well (and while I may write a number of things in the forthcoming pages that are open to question, this claim is true). When we first demonstrated the Caulk-Rite tool to contractors and retailers at home improvement trade shows, we would hear audible gasps from our primarily male audience. These reactions confirmed we had a winner. And unlike Andrew's soaker tub, this invention was indeed "small, cheap, plastic and mass-marketable."

Andrew Dewberry
with the Caulk-Rite
tool that started it all

When asked to recall the early days of the Vancouver Tool Corporation (VTC), which Andrew established to sell the Caulk-Rite tool, I can't provide many details. At the time, Andrew was visiting various manufacturers and exploring the patenting process, I was very much caught up in completing my Ph.D. and dealing with the politics of academic life. I knew he was inventing, but this was nothing new. He had always invented. Our telephone pad was full of scribbled objects he had thought up, and wherever we lived he was an active member of the local inventors' society.

In fact, all the men I've known seem to have had some sort of bizarre hobby or interest. During my childhood my father spent all his spare moments in the garage, restoring vintage cars, which we then took to car shows every weekend. I never rode in a modern car until I was 10, and I thought everyone waved at you when you rode by, just like in *Chitty Chitty Bang*

Bang. Past boyfriends had been passionate about Tolkien, soccer, model cars, independence for Kashmir, frogs and Black Sabbath. My female friends, by contrast, did not and do not today have the same range of interests. My father had an expression: "All men need somewhere to sulk." The garage was his place, and I had interpreted this gem of wisdom to mean a space that was not necessarily physical. Andrew's inventing space was partly mental—an area without me, non-threatening and harmless but needed for his and our overall well-being. Funding for the prototypes of Andrew's inventions came from his occasional architectural consulting jobs; it was cash we regarded as extra and not needed for the necessities of mortgage and food.

So until one evening in 1996, Andrew's inventing was a hobby that did not affect me. It was when I found boxes containing 3,000 plastic handles, 3,000 rubber blades, 5,000 backing cards and 5,000 plastic package covers on our living room floor (and heard the casual comment, "We can put them together after dinner") that I realized Andrew's hobby had taken a totally new direction while I had been busy with my academic life.

And I *had* been busy. Since obtaining my Ph.D. the year before, I had taught four courses in the criminology and

The Caulk-Rite
assembly plant
(our living room)

Assembling the first
3,000 Caulk-Rite tools

sociology departments at SFU, written a 300-page textbook on policing in Canada, undertaken a six-month research project for the Aboriginal Policing Directorate of the federal Solicitor General, which involved travelling in the Northwest Territories and the Hudson Bay area, and started to research a book on campgrounds in B.C. Despite all these commitments I sat on the floor with Andrew after dinner each night for three months, assembling and packaging Caulk-Rite tools and listening to CBC radio (we had no TV). At times my fingers bled because some forcing was required to get the unevenly cut rubber blades into the plastic tool handle. On July 12, 1996, we sold the first six Caulk-Rite tools to a Home Hardware store near our house for $12—a milestone. I went to the liquor store and bought champagne. That night we didn't assemble tools but celebrated by eating cheese fondue on the porch and discussing how to grow our new business and spend the profits. We decided we would buy Tahiti and rename it Caulkiti.

This initial, albeit limited, success made me believe that it would be easy to sell our product to the champions of the home improvement industry—Canadian Tire (441 stores), Home Hardware (1,068 stores), Home Depot (67 stores) and RONA (484 stores). Andrew fuelled this belief by constantly reiterating that *everyone* needed the Caulk-Rite tool, and I believed in my husband and listened to his arguments. But we knew nothing about these retail giants, or about the industry itself, which is where my research background helped.

The North American home improvement industry

By inventing a product for the home improvement industry and not, for example, for the record player, we had chosen a consumer area that was burgeoning. I knew nothing of this industry but soon found the information required.

There are a number of Canadian magazines dedicated to the industry, such as *Hardware Merchandising*, *Home Improvement Retailing* and *Canadian Contractor*. There are even more publications in the United States (for example, *Do-It-Yourself Retailing*, *Home Improvement Market*, *Paint Dealer*) and Europe (*DIY In Europe*, *DIY Business*). These allowed us to learn about the industry and the major industry players. They also told us which retailers were acquiring which competitors, listed trade shows and gave projected and existing sales for the big companies as well as overall trends in the marketplace. Following are examples of the type of data provided:

- According to Statistics Canada, the average amount spent by Canadian households in 2002 on home renovation and repairs was $2,910. Four years earlier the figure was $1,837.
- The Canadian Mortgage and Housing Corporation forecasts consumers will spend $33.5 billion in 2004 on home renovations, an increase from $32.1 billion in 2003 and $29.8 billion in 2002.
- According to *Hardware Merchandising*, Canada's retail and building-supply industry has grown 7.18% on average in the last nine years.

- In 2003 the home improvement market in the United States saw a 5% growth to achieve a volume of $208 billion. This 5% annual growth is expected to continue until at least 2007.
- Gross margins made by hardware stores in 2002 averaged 40%. For larger home improvement stores the figure was 30%.
- In the U.S. sales are controlled by three big players, Home Depot (sales of $54.2 billion in 2001), Lowe's ($26.5 billion in 2001) and Menards ($5.3 billion in 2001).
- In Canada over 22% of home improvement sales come from 170 big box stores operated by RONA (including Reno Depot), Home Depot and Kent (with Home Depot controlling 64% of these). Canadian Tire has a further 15% of the entire market share.
- According to Statistics Canada in 2002, $375.7 million of hardware, home renovation and gardening products was sold through non-retail outlets (the Internet and television infomercials, for example), an increase of 2% from 2001.
- Women are increasingly involved in home renovation projects. By 2010 an estimated 28% of North American households will be headed by women.

This information therefore showed us:

- We would be placing our product in a growth market.
- Retailers would expect gross margins of 30% to 40%.
- Who the key players in Canada are.
- Who the key players in the United States are.
- We should explore using infomercials to sell our product.
- We should market to women.

In reading the trade literature we soon became acquainted with the home improvement industry from a safe arm's-length perspective. But as the rest of our story shows, there is a chasm of difference between *reading* about Home Depot and *selling* to Home Depot.

From criminology to caulking

You do not have to read the next bit. It contains the personal stuff—the background that *I* think is important but that some readers may see as irrelevant to the story of an inventor. I have included it because in running a small business I have come to realize that the buyers and others we encounter on a day-to-day basis want to deal with "Jayne and Andrew." I've learned that business, even a caulking-tool business, is all about personal relationships and that we *are* VTC. It is people as well as products that are important. I've also included this background to show how happenstance—those chance occurrences in life—can have very cogent effects on your destiny. Academic business courses aren't the only way to provide the knowledge and instill the drive that the inventor-entrepreneur must have. Life can be the best teacher of all.

How we stumbled into being Canada's largest manufacturer of caulking tools began in January 1982 when I was offered a job teaching English to French businessmen in Lyon. I was delighted with this offer, which came after I had been living in France for six months as an au pair. I returned to England to make arrangements to move and while there received two telephone calls. The first came from a member of the Rotary Club, the men's business organization. Prior to completing my undergraduate degree I had explored the possibility of undertaking a master's degree in criminology in Canada and had approached the Rotary Foundation for a scholarship. The Rotarian who called was very persuasive, saying there were not enough applicants for this scholarship and I really should apply. A couple of days later I received the second telephone call, informing me that the position in Lyon was no longer available, so I applied for and was granted the scholarship.

In 1984 I moved to Ottawa and began a two-year program for a master's degree in criminology. I graduated in 1985, having completed the course in the shortest time in the 15-year history of the program, and returned to England. There I married Andrew and worked as a researcher until 1991, when I left to start my Ph.D. studies in Vancouver.

From the beginning of my academic career I had wanted to earn a decent salary (not a ton of money) and enjoy a stable conservative life. But primarily I yearned to espouse various criminological theories, deliver lectures to crowds of undergraduates, share research findings with contemporaries at academic conferences, publish empirical masterpieces that students could not understand but would be forced to read, and travel to far-away places and argue the latest theories with fellow academics. In order to do this, I made sure I wrote extensively and published in practitioner and academic publications. I taught a number of different courses and received excellent evaluations. I did everything I was told to do by the tenured members of the university community to ensure a successful academic career. Once I had completed my Ph.D. I applied for 13 jobs in North America and without exception was short-listed for an interview. At the time, Andrew had just established the Vancouver Tool Corporation and we wanted to stay in B.C., so I decided to wait until a position came up locally. In April 1996 a three-year contract for an assistant professor at SFU was advertised. The advertisement read "a Ph.D. is required." Nineteen people applied for the post: 11 women (all with Ph.D.s) and 8 men. Four men were short-listed for an interview, three without a Ph.D.

I was furious. I couldn't help but feel that the appointments committee had ignored its own clearly stated academic requirements in order to select its preferred candidate. I protested, knowing that doing so would likely amount to academic suicide: never again would I be able to obtain an untainted academic reference from the school of criminology at SFU. Given my excellent academic, publications, and teaching records, I could not fathom why the appointments committee would find these other people to be more qualified than me.

For two years this experience ate away at me, and I would lay awake at night visiting and revisiting the perceived injustice. I have subsequently heard many similar stories from friends who work in academic and other large institutions. While not mitigating the hurt in any way or making the rejection easier to accept, these testimonials have made me appreciate that this was not an isolated or even unusual experience.

Nearly 10 years later, I still marvel over what I see as a cynical attitude in the academic world. I know of professors who drop into their offices no more than once a week, who offer research contracts to their relatives, and who avoid attending conferences or publishing new material. I often wonder whether I too would have become so cynical had I remained in academia. Instead, I now enjoy an enviable income, I work my own hours in our comfortable home, spend as much time with my children as I want, and enjoy a quality of life that would have been impossible on an assistant professor's salary and schedule. In the end, an experience that was without a doubt devastating to me led to the successful formation of VTC.

The fate factors

The university experience was the first of several "fate factors" that influenced the growth of VTC. The second was our desire to start a family. In October 1994 I found out I was pregnant; 12 weeks later I had a miscarriage, and six months later I repeated the experience. At the time I knew of no one who had miscarried, but as I told more and more people, both men and women, I found the experience to be extremely common. Following my second miscarriage we started the long three-year round of exhausting and intrusive tests in which every gynecologist and his or her student stared up my vagina and prodded every part of my body. While this was going on, Andrew would invariably be talking to the medical staff about the vast array of implements and devices they were employing and how the equipment might be modified, improved or completely reinvented to obtain the tissue/blood/hormone sample desired. Consequently Andrew found these visits to B.C.'s Women's Hospital much more stimulating than I ever did.

In January 1998, following four years of tests, my gynecologist suggested in vitro fertilization (IVF), which would cost between $5,000 and $7,000 per attempt, money we did not have but could perhaps have found. We decided to stop trying and trust a fate that had determined we would be members of that affluent and childless group. We drove to Tofino on the west coast of Vancouver Island, walked on the wind-swept beach, got drunk, had sex because we wanted to and not because it was the "right time" and cried a lot. The dream of children was not obtainable and it was time to move on. I did not look back. Four months later, following a trade show selling caulking tools in Chicago, we got drunk on blue-lagoon cocktails and later that night Jack was conceived. Acknowledging to ourselves that we would remain childless had reduced our stress, and this facilitated the conception. It is a story I have subsequently heard from many other couples who, like us, suffered the trauma of infertility.

We know now that if we had had a child in the summer of 1995 we would not have had VTC. The two gorgeous boys we are now lucky enough to parent have tremendous advantages in having parents, albeit older ones, who have the finances and the time to respond to their demands. They have never known the routine of dad leaving for the office and mum staying at home. They believe that "going to work" means descending to the basement to invent something or to use a computer to sell something.

The period from early 1996 until Jack's birth in January 1999 was crucial for the development of VTC. If we had not suffered the miscarriages, I would not have been able to dedicate the time (about six hours a day) required to market the caulking tools; we would not have been free to travel to trade shows or spend hours discussing the new venture and feeding off each other's enthusiasm. Thus events we found painful and challenging ultimately supported VTC's growth.

The importance of personality

There were, of course, other factors that contributed to the successful growth of our business—not the least of which was our personalities. While I have not read a vast number of business books, the ones I have perused suggest that anyone contemplating establishing a business should determine whether they have what it takes. These books often ask the would-be entrepreneur questions such as "Do you like working by yourself?" and "Are you happy working long hours?" A question far more relevant when it comes to inventors is "Do you believe you can successfully market your invention?" Over the last nine years I have counselled countless inventors who wanted to know "how we did it." Most inventors are not marketers, and Andrew is a good example of this.

Andrew is extremely clever but also very quiet. At high school he was probably the brightest of 400 students. In his final year at high school he was off for four months with pleurisy, a debilitating lung disease, but he still managed to obtain straight As and a place to study architecture at Bristol, a prestigious English university. He is a qualified architect in both Canada and the United Kingdom. He is almost six feet tall, the fourth of six children, and (I think) relatively good-looking. He is one of those men whom women instinctively trust and warm to and not at all "one of the boys." He speaks quietly, and at parties I love to watch his audience get closer and closer to him, trying to grasp what he says. No one hates him and he hates no one. He reasons well, is unemotional (I was with him for 10 years before I saw him shed a tear) and knows what he wants. He is methodical, patient and practical. He is the inventor in our partnership and within the company deals with computer issues, lawyers, patents, copyrights, trademarks, product modification, insurance, suppliers, quality control and, of course, new product development.

By contrast, I am not quiet. While I am more of an extrovert than Andrew, I do not get on with everyone. I frequently rub people the wrong way. I have no patience. I get bored easily and get emotional even more easily. I am not intuitively clever and have to work and study hard for what I want. I am the marketer in our partnership and within VTC I invoice customers, pay bills, undertake all sales and promotion, and do the schmoozing—a big part of business. My advice to any would-be inventor is to examine whether you can, in fact, market your own invention. Most of the inventors I have met cannot. The success of VTC can be attributed in large part to the complementary personal characteristics that Andrew and I brought to the business.

The importance of time and place

Two other factors contributing to our success that must be acknowledged are the optimistic economic climate of the 1990s and the Canadian society in which we found ourselves. We had left a country with a rigid class structure and come to the "land of opportunity," where you could speak your dreams and people would not laugh at you or say you would inevitably fail. In our experience, Canadians were inclined to express such unbridled enthusiasm when hearing of our ambitions that we sometimes wondered if they had ulterior motives. In 1999 I read an article in *The Economist* that described the reaction of three cultures to starting a new business: in China all your relatives start to work for you to make sure the business succeeds; in North America friends and relatives offer financial support; but in Britain they tell you the business will fail, then when it does not they scratch your car. We could not have started VTC in England: the negativity, cynicism and skepticism of the society and our family and friends would have been too great. Although I find it difficult to be critical of my birth country—there are many things I adore in the culture—the cynicism that is almost endemic in England is not conducive to inventing or entrepreneurship. A Toronto friend who has watched VTC grow says we definitely fall into the "new immigrant" category—arriving with nothing, working initially in dead-end jobs (Andrew started off in Canada like so many others, doing telephone sales), living in a one-bedroom apartment, doing without luxuries and working hard to build our new life. The Canadian environment offered us so many opportunities and stimulated our creativity; had we tried to realize our potential in England during the Margaret Thatcher years, we would have been stifled.

As it was, we did not avoid all negativity. When we had a party at our house in the summer of 1996 and I was asked what I planned to do with our Caulk-Rite tools, I told a senior marketing director who worked for Telus and a friend involved in construction industry sales that I planned to market them myself. Both looked stony-faced and explained that marketing was very difficult work and I could not just start without any formal training. They suggested I continue my career as an academic. Little did these two men know that they had thrown down a gauntlet that I was about to pick up.

Advice for the inventor

1. If you have a number of inventions you could take to market, choose the one that is "small, cheap, plastic and mass-marketable."

2. Read the industry and consumer literature for the market you want to enter. Find trade magazines and learn as much as possible about your market.

3. Ask yourself whether you may regret, perhaps for the rest of your life, not trying to take your invention forward.

4. Critically review whether you are the right person and have the right attributes to promote and sell your invention. If you are not, then you will need to explore other ways to sell your idea (e.g., by hiring a marketing company). Alternatively, you might find a partner who has the attributes needed to market your invention, keeping in mind that inventors are inveterate "tinkerers" but marketers need to work with a finished final product.

5. Consider whether this is the correct time in your life to develop a new business.

6. Determine whether you have the required emotional and personal support networks in place. Does your family sanction your new venture? Will they give you the time and financial resources required to make it a success?

7. Consider whether you have the physical space to produce, package, and store your invention.

8. Consider whether you have the correct systems in place (computer, fax, email, telephone, etc.) to start a business.

9. Determine whether your community and the current economic climate are conducive to launching a new business and a new invention in your chosen market.

CHAPTER 2: **From Prototype to Product**

The Importance of People

Our basement has always been full of tools and devices to assist the inventing process. I do not know what these things are or what they do, but I am invariably told that the inventor needs more of them. While Andrew was developing Caulk-Rite he was working with a number of prototypes carved from pink Styrofoam. During the time he was carving, we had pink crumbs littering every corner of our house. Once he had a rough idea of how the tool would look, he made another prototype from acrylic sheet, which he glued and bent, using the oven to assist in the process.

The learning curve we followed once Andrew moved from these prototypes to a finished product was steep but enjoyable. We soon found that existing businesses with expertise were more than willing to help us. We also learned that while ideas are easy, especially for an inventor, deciding which ones are profitable and should be taken to the next stage involves researching just how much it will cost to take this leap.

After we had a prototype we learned that we had to do the following:

- Find out how much the tooling for mass production of the product would be.
- Determine the costs of packaging.
- Determine the costs of patenting.
- Estimate the cost of production per unit and set a price.

But without a doubt the biggest lesson we learned was that people are key and choosing the right suppliers makes all the difference.

Tool development

At first Andrew had wanted to make his caulking tool in metal. When he realized this would be too costly, he began looking for plastic injection-mold manufacturers in the phone directory. Men at the first two firms he approached spent hours with him. I have since learned that everybody (not just me) loves an inventor, not necessarily because they see the inventor as a future customer but because manufacturers want to offer their technical advice and experience and rise to the challenge an inventor presents. The guidance Andrew received from these men was priceless. It could not have been found in books. We continue to buy from one of the companies, despite being able to purchase more cheaply elsewhere. We like this small family-run supplier, whose owner at the outset spent so much time guiding the development of the new product and who saw Caulk-Rite as his baby as much as ours. It is a personal as well as a business connection (they have photographs of our children and samples of the caulking tools in their office display cabinets).

In developing the Caulk-Rite blade, Andrew again went through the phone directory in search of local suppliers. During these approaches he frequently heard, "It's not the sort of thing

The inventor in
his workshop

we do, but have you tried ... " He spent evenings driving to warehouse units in far-away, difficult-to-find industrial areas, visiting various manufacturers and describing what he wanted, but without giving too much away since the patents were not yet in place. Again he was given feedback and advice, all free of charge.

We have developed a very personal relationship with all of our suppliers. In the beginning they knew we were just starting out, had limited finances, did not know about business and had no idea how to sell tools. We were that "weird, enthusiastic inventing couple with the English accents," and without exception our suppliers believed in us and supported us. And as VTC became more profitable, we in turn supported them. Although Andrew was initially nervous about approaching these companies, he need not have been. Without exception everyone was accommodating to his needs. Almost all were also immigrants to Canada.

Once the Caulk-Rite tool had been perfected, costly molds were commissioned. Next we had to name the tool. The "naming" process had been an informal discussion involving the two of us for a long time, and it soon became formalized as we wandered around hardware stores to look at the names, packages, and colours of other products. "Rite" was often used (Paint-Rite, Plumb-Rite, etc.) and naturally joined "Caulk" to form the name of our tool. We then decided that our Caulk-Rite tool should be molded from red plastic because this would make it similar to other hardware-store products (unlike pink plastic, which wouldn't be typical) yet allow it to stand out in the sometimes dimly lit aisles of big box retailers.

Packaging, assembly, and pricing

After developing and naming our tool, the next issue to be explored was presentation. I had never thought packaging was that important, but it is *vital*, especially for a new invention. We now spend more on packaging and assembly than we do on the Caulk-Rite and Caulk-Away tools themselves. Initially we did not see packaging as so important. Andrew had chosen our printer after hearing him speak to the B.C. Inventors Society. He was one of the owners of a local family-run business and we found him to be very friendly and approachable. A student working for the firm was taking a college course in graphic design, so we had this individual put the hand-drawn graphics together for $100. The printing was two-colour because we were unable to afford full colour. We added instructions in English and French for the Canadian market and obtained bar codes and had them placed at the required size on the packaging. We selected a "slide blister"— a plastic sleeve that could be slipped over the backing card to hold the tool—so that we could do the assembly ourselves and not have to pay more for a ready-glued card and stick-on blister. Once Caulk-Rite started to sell, retailers told us they did not like this slide-blister packaging, because the tools could be too easily removed, so we quickly changed to the stick-on blister.

After receiving positive feedback from our first two trade shows we decided it was time to invest in decent packaging and commission a graphic design firm (see more about this in Chapter 3). We made telephone calls to firms of various sizes and explained what we wanted, then met with them. Quotes came in ranging from $3,000 to $20,000. The highest quote came from an agency that wanted to charge us $2,000 for walking around hardware stores and researching the home-improvement industry. A more reasonable quote came from a guy working from his home, who seemed nice enough when we met with him one morning. When we returned a few days later to finalize things, he smelled strongly of alcohol and had a couple of final-demand bills on his desk that he made no effort to hide. We made excuses and left. After we relayed the story to our blister manufacturer, he told us of a company that wasn't too "arty" and specialized in graphics for the food/hardware industry. We soon met one of the partners and liked his personal style and relaxed yet professional manner. The firm has worked with us ever since and is now one of the most successful graphic design agencies in B.C. Again, it was our initial attraction to one individual and his ability to understand us that cemented the relationship.

Our packaging has two languages on the front (English and French) and three on the back (we added Spanish for the U.S. market). When we sell tools to Europe and to customers who want to sell them under their own name, we supply a disk containing all the graphics and instructions so the customer does not need to have photographs taken or translations made.

A number of our tools require that a rubber blade be inserted into a plastic body. This assembly work is undertaken by home workers contracted by our assembl y firm. Tools and blades are delivered to the supplier, who in turn takes them to the homes of his employees. The packaging and boxing of

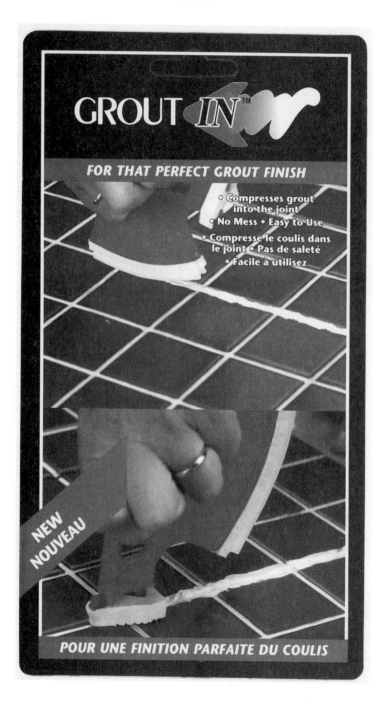

products is undertaken by the same company that does our printing. A few years ago we packaged our tools in boxes of 50, but we received pressure from our customers to package in sub-cartons of 10 and master cartons of 50. This added considerably to our costs but made our customers happier.

Setting a price is another part of keeping customers (and you) happy. The business literature suggests there are two ways to determine the price of a product. The first method involves calculating all your costs, both production and overhead (office, freight, legal expenses, insurance, salaries, etc.) and adding a percentage for profit. The second method involves choosing a price you think the product should be sold for, based on what is already being charged in the marketplace for similar products, and working backwards to determine whether all your costs will be covered. For example, if you believe your product should sell for $4.50 and you know the retailer will want at least 50%, you will need to determine if you can manufacture your product for $2.25 and still cover all costs and make a profit. VTC chose the second method when deciding on price, and in nine years we have never needed to increase the prices of any of our tools. In our case, production costs have decreased as production runs have increased.

The advantages of local production

One question we are often asked is why we do not manufacture our little plastic tools offshore. First, we benefit from selling Canadian products to the Canadian market, especially to customers such as Canadian Tire, Home Hardware, and RONA, who all profess to be "Proudly Canadian" and want to purchase Canadian-made items. Second, while we might save some money producing offshore, we would have to order an entire container-load of products and could suffer serious supply problems in the event of port strikes in Vancouver or shipping disruptions in other parts of the world. Major headaches would ensue if we could not meet agreed-upon delivery dates, and companies such as Canadian Tire would charge financial penalties.

By using local suppliers VTC has established a fantastic reputation for shipping all quantities required on time and for paying our suppliers within 30 days (I would prefer to see the money in their pockets than at our bank). Having established solid relationships also means that if we do get an urgent order we can usually just make a telephone call and our suppliers will do everything in their power to deliver what we need. By producing locally we can also confidently order custom-designed tools with different colours and logos and have them made quickly.

And the advantage of being in close geographical contact with your supplier can never be underestimated. A couple of years ago I had a telephone call from one of our injection molders telling me the Caulk-Away tool was a little "orange" because the machine had been running overnight without enough red pigment. We had a long discussion about whether this "orange" was in fact "orange" and not "red" and whether it mattered. After this circular discussion had gone on for rather a long time I decided to drive over to the plant and take a look: the tools were fine and only slightly less red than usual—no one other than the producer would notice. Now if I had received a telephone call from Asia saying the tools were slightly orange, this would not have been resolved so easily—and who knows whether I would have received this call at all.

Local suppliers can also be an excellent source of referrals: printers know packagers, packagers know blister manufacturers, blister manufacturers have customers who, like us, are trying to understand how to sell to Canadian

Superstore. There is a fantastic network to access and not through the traditional channels. Also, if a printing firm, for example, recommends a packaging company you know they can work together. In addition, we have found the ethnic diversity of our suppliers to be a real bonus. We deal with a vast array of Canadians who originate from every corner of the globe. These first-, second- and third-generation Canadians are enthusiastically building their own small businesses and are happy to share the wealth of knowledge they have gained in Canada and abroad.

The advantages of a home-based business

VTC is still run with just Andrew and me from the basement of our home. Someone recently described us as a "virtual business—like Nike" in that we contract out everything and leave those companies who specialize in packaging, warehousing, injection molds, assembly, and so on to do the work that they know well. In this respect our company is an organizational one. Our workdays are spent on organizational tasks: shipping tools to respond to purchase orders; responding to inquiries; ordering products; and, when time permits, deciding on the next promotional initiative. We use accounting software to keep track of sales, purchase orders, invoices, accounts receivable, and accounts payable, although I still keep a large envelope in my "in" tray with the words "Unpaid Invoices YAK!" written on it. At times we have thought about getting a warehouse (Andrew would love to drive around in a forklift all day) but have decided we would end up with too many headaches for the small saving gained. We currently rent warehouse space from our packaging supplier, which is ideal because he has the facility to ship full pallets of products. We usually visit the warehouse once a week.

A few years ago I was acutely embarrassed about working from home and would try not to tell suppliers or customers. As we have grown and I have realized that a lot of the professionals we deal with also work from home, this embarrassment has eased. I have learned that buyers for big retailers do not care where our office is located. They are only concerned that Vancouver Tool can supply a quality product on time and at an agreed-upon price (with generous discounts, of course).

There are considerable advantages in operating our business from home. These include not having to commute, not having to dress in a certain way, and not having to keep to someone else's schedule. We can work our own hours. With two young children (we had VTC before we had the children) this is a real advantage. We are easily able to respond if they are ill and need our attention, and in the summer months we can end our days early and take family trips to the beach and then work late into the evening if required. In addition there are considerable financial benefits in operating the business from home. Our profitability as a company would decrease considerably if we had to pay to rent and furnish office space.

Receiving 40,000
Caulk-Rite tools

In working from home it is important to establish a defined space that is dedicated to the operation of your business. Our basement is our workspace with Andrew's Invention Room (the envy of all his male friends), a storage room, and our large office. By descending the basement stairs we become VTC workers. When climbing out of the basement we are Mum and Dad—Jayne and Andrew—again. This distinction is important for our business and personal lives.

Essential professional services and connections

There are times when you must use professionals and times when you do not need their services. For instance, we use a professional photographer for all our promotional photographs, but we do not use a hand model. As soon as we learned that a hand model costs $200 per hour, we decided that my hands (smaller and less hairy than Andrew's) could be treated to a $25 manicure and then be featured holding the tools for our promotional literature.

For the inventor, the most costly professional is undoubtedly the patent lawyer. Our legal expenses are ongoing and considerable. We have five full patents in Canada and the United States and five full or pending patents in many other countries (we do not have patents in jurisdictions such as China or Russia, where there is no point because of lack of enforcement). This is an expense that the inventor has to accept. These patents supply us with the protection we and our distributors need to grow and develop our business and prevent counterfeit tools from entering the markets we have secured.

We often hear would-be inventors say they plan to "flood the market" with their revolutionary device, sell millions and get a name for themselves rather than going the costly route of filing for patent protection. While this may be an option, it requires placing the invention in stores and getting it accepted by large retail buyers. Even the inventor with the most awesome better mousetrap and a ton of money will find this difficult. To be able to "flood the market" you have to get into the market first.

When Andrew started VTC he wrote the Caulk-Rite patent himself, drawing on the expertise available at Patscan, a professional service for patent research based at the University of British Columbia. (At the time, you could not undertake a patent search via the Internet, which is how patents are researched today.) To save costs he authored and submitted the Caulk-Rite patent knowing it could be altered at a later date once sales created the funds to pay the fees. Now everything related to VTC patents and their upkeep is handled by our lawyers. This is a very expensive and at times inexplicable process. Andrew still undertakes the initial patent search, writes a short history of the invention and does a sketch of the attributes of the invention. By doing this he learns more about the product and simplifies the sketch of attributes so that there is less work for the lawyer. This has the dual benefit of lowering the lawyer's fees while increasing the clarity of the application. We chose a law firm that specializes in patent law and has excellent international connections. Over the last nine years our lawyers have defended us in two cases of patent infringement, one in the United States and one in Germany. Successful prosecutions were conducted in both cases; however, the legal costs of doing so outweighed the financial compensation obtained. Still, if you are in production for the long-term you need the patent protection.

We also use professionals for product liability insurance, which we must have, and a multitude of other kinds of insurance. From 2003 to 2004 our insurance fees increased by 500% because of the increased trade we did with the United

States and its policies following 9/11. We have known our extremely approachable accountant since we first arrived in Canada. We value him as an advisor, confidant, and friend.

We have not been so lucky with all our professional connections. When we were in the initial stages of launching VTC I went to see a small business advisor funded by the B.C. provincial government. After I showed him a somewhat rudimentary business plan, he spent 20 minutes telling me our business would fail because it had not been properly thought out. He suggested I return to academia (while still managing to convey his belief that I would be just as unsuccessful there). I felt quite dejected after this meeting, despite telling myself that this advisor was a government bureaucrat who might not know what he was talking about. Unfortunately, when things were not going well this charmless man's words would punctuate my consciousness.

I had more success with Industry Canada, the federal government agency responsible for promoting Canadian businesses in the international marketplace. Although I have found the quality of Industry Canada staff in foreign countries varies significantly (some are brilliant and go out of their way to help; others are less diligent), they have generally been helpful. One representative in the United States even attended sales meetings with buyers on our behalf. Another organized a trip to Seattle for Canadian manufacturers in the hardware industry to acquaint them with the United States market and the process of exporting. In early 1997 Andrew and I travelled to Seattle for this extremely useful two-day event, and in March 1999 we were awarded the Exporter of the Month award by Industry Canada. While I do not think VTC was entirely deserving of this award (Industry Canada had a shortage of firms to recognize at the time) it did serve as good publicity for us.

I must mention one other important connection. Andrew has always been a member of a brilliant networking group full of characters—the B.C. Inventors Society (or, as I call it, the Mad Inventors Society). From 2001 to 2004 Andrew served as president of this primarily male group of between 30 and 60 active members. While most members have ideas rather than solid inventions with patent pending, the society has proved to be an important connection for VTC. Through the society we have been introduced to injection mold makers, printers, and marketers, and have had access to the minds and opinions of other inventors—yet another example of the importance of people when it comes to taking your idea forward.

Advice for the inventor

1. Visit stores you think could be interested in stocking your product to look at related items and learn what they have been named and how they have been packaged and promoted.
2. Contact at least four companies you might want to use for packaging and graphics. Decide whether you can work with a particular company by meeting with the people involved.
3. Consider using local production facilities, at least initially, when you begin manufacturing your product.
4. If working from home, ensure you create a defined physical space from which to run your business.
5. Do not make the mistake of believing you can successfully "flood the market" with your product unless you have a number of large purchase orders from several major retailers and a lot of money to fill these orders.
6. Choose a good patent lawyer if you are serious about your invention and its growth potential.
7. Contact government officials both in Canada and abroad (web sites are a good place to start) if you are thinking of exporting.
8. Meet with any networking groups (societies for inventors, business associations) that may be relevant to developing, marketing, and selling your invention.

Persistence Pays Off

In September 1996, following our initial sale of six Caulk-Rite tools to a local Home Hardware store, we travelled to northern B.C. and the Yukon with two research goals: to find out about campgrounds for a book I was writing on camping in B.C. and to learn about the market for caulking tools. We called on every Home Hardware, Pro Hardware, small independent do-it-yourself retailer, and large lumberyard we passed on this 4,300-mile (7,000-kilometre) journey. We left countless samples of Caulk-Rite and spoke to many retailers. Each night we camped in a provincial park campground. Just like travelling salesmen in the Depression, we rattled along all kinds of roads with a box of tools in the trunk, selling to every far-flung community we found. The Caulk-Rite tool was cheap enough to give away and that's what we did. My advice to any inventor would be to do this if you can. A new item sits on someone's desk or workbench and is shown to others with pride. In the hardware industry this item is often tested by those who may one day sell it. We learned a lot by talking to these small-town retailers who, unlike their busy Vancouver counterparts, had time to offer their expertise and opinions. We also frequently got to speak to the owners of these stores, the individuals responsible for making the purchasing decisions. Upon returning to Vancouver I contacted these retailers and received orders and feedback.

Talking to those in the industry, especially about the marketing of a product and the competition you might face, can teach you so much. While the inventor may know the product intimately, it is the retailer who will be promoting and endorsing it. Inventors must accept the fact that they are going to have to work with these people and should acknowledge their comments, whether relevant or not. Too many inventors are reluctant to accept criticism and they end up missing out on useful advice from others, especially those who have an in-depth knowledge of the trade.

Preliminary research

Before we began our northern research tour, Andrew and I attended the B.C. Home Show specifically to approach a man named Shell Busey, a home-renovation specialist who hosts TV and radio shows. Our aim was to find out what was "out there." When Andrew asked Shell how to apply caulk around a bathtub, he laboriously explained the process and advised using a finger soaked in dish detergent to apply the sealant. Andrew asked if there was a tool available (we had seen hard plastic tools in some stores but had been told by the retailers selling them that they did not work). Shell said there were some things on the market, but a finger was still the best option. If anyone knew what was available, it was Shell Busey. Our own research findings were confirmed.

After our three-week trip we returned to Vancouver, where Andrew went back to the hassles of working at UBC and I made a list of all the independent home improvement retailers in the Greater Vancouver area to supplement the list I had made on our travels. One late-September morning I drove Andrew to work, kissed him goodbye and then proceeded very nervously to a Home Hardware store. I spoke to the owner, showed him the tool, and he agreed to take 10. I immediately telephoned Andrew with the news and we glowed down the telephone line at each other. The sale of 10 tools was the start of something wonderful. By the end of the day I had sold 40 Caulk-Rite tools to six Home Hardware stores and had left samples at another 10 stores. At the same time I contacted the Big Buyer for all the Home Hardware stores, who is based in St. Jacobs, Ontario. While interested in Caulk-Rite, he was not prepared to purchase large quantities or put it in the three Home Hardware warehouses, where it could be used to fill orders from independent dealers. He was polite and encouraging and explained that if I got enough interest from individual retailers he might commit to it. This was my introduction to the complicated mind of the hardware-store buyer, who is cautious and conservative and does not like to take risks. As the inventor of a new product you must prove the worth of your product to the buyer before he (and for the most part it is a "he" in the hardware industry) will even consider taking a chance on it.

Over the next six months I called the St. Jacobs Home Hardware buyer every time one of his 1,000-plus stores listed my product. I spoke to him directly or left messages explaining precisely which retailer had accepted the product and how many were ordered. Just before Christmas 1996 I excitedly called to let the Big Buyer know I had my first repeat order. At this time I was making no money whatsoever from these labour-intensive sales, having to deliver or ship fewer than 20 tools and invoice for less than $50. My regular calls to St. Jacobs got to be a joke, but one with an important message. I would say to the buyer, "Hi. It's me again, just to let you know I sold another six tools to a Home Hardware dealer today. Hope you're still considering Caulk-Rite. Thanks!"

At the same time I was approaching Home Hardware, I was also courting other big players. The Vancouver Public Library yielded industry journals (*Hardware Merchandising, Home Improvement Retailing*) that taught me some of the biggest players were in Ontario and Quebec and did not have a large retail presence in B.C. We devised a buyer contact sheet (see Appendix 1) for the name, address, and telephone number of each buyer in the major hardware chains we were chasing. Many of the larger chains have different buyers for different categories of products, and it is important to speak to the correct one. We learned that Caulk-Rite generally fell into the "paint sundry items" category and that most large chains had a buyer for this area.

A lamb among the wolves

Thus began my long (and not always happy) relationship with buyers. Once I found out the name of the person I needed to approach, I telephoned to introduce myself,

At last!
Caulk-Rite appears
in the stores of a large
Canadian retail chain

then sent samples of the Caulk-Rite tool together with a covering letter (see Appendix 2). After a couple of weeks I called to learn the buyer's reaction. I got nowhere. Buyers did not want to buy from a company that they had never heard of, that was from the other side of the country, that had no track record and that was a "one-SKU vendor" (SKU referring to stock-keeping unit or product). They also did not want anything to do with a product that was encased in really bad two-colour packaging (and it was *really* bad). They also complained that the product was too expensive (a standard response I have since learned every buyer memorizes in Buying 101 at business school and tells all vendors, no matter who they are or what they are selling). The buyers did not feel there was any need for the tool (What else would you use your finger for?) and basically wanted to get my naïve and overenthusiastic English voice and "that pathetic little plastic tool" away from their desk and out of their lives. This was a very depressing time. I *hated* making these approaches and receiving such negative responses. It is easy to understand why so many novice entrepreneurs give up at this stage.

Luckily, it was not all bad. During this exhausting round of telephone calls there were a few individuals who gave me advice and encouragement. One told me about distributors—companies that buy tools from a small manufacturer such as VTC, mark up the price by 30% and sell the item to the larger retailers. This relationship reduces the headaches for the manufacturer, who no longer has to approach uncommunicative buyers, and benefits the retailer, who no longer has to deal with hundreds of "little guys." A gorgeous man called Brian spent ages describing the process to me one wet November afternoon. He was a buyer for a chain of stores based in B.C. and he explained that he would not buy directly from me but *would* buy through a distributor. He recommended two to me, including one in Ontario that turned out to be the largest distributor of paint sundry items. When I called this firm—Dynamic Paint Products—I initiated what was to become one of our most profitable relationships.

At about the same time, I telephoned the Independent Lumber Dealers Association and spoke to a man about my difficulties getting the Caulk-Rite tool in front of the buyers and into the marketplace. He spent ages offering advice and guidance in a really sensitive and not at all condescending manner. Two years later I was in Toronto accepting an award for our second product, Caulk-Away. I was nervously clutching a glass of white wine and trying (unsuccessfully) not to feel out of place as one of the very few women in a huge presentation hall. Suddenly I spotted a badge with a name I recognized—the man from the Independent Lumber Dealers Association who had been so helpful. I went over to him and started to explain who I was, but he stopped me mid-sentence and said of course he remembered me because at the end of the telephone call he had replaced the handset and thought to himself, "There goes a lamb among the wolves." Since he made that comment, I have always thought of VTC as a lamb finding its way in the world.

Our first trade show

It was during this early stage of foraging for information (where my background as a researcher undoubtedly came in handy) that I learned of the now-defunct Western Hardware Show, a trade show for the hardware industry held in Vancouver. At this show exhibitors were given the opportunity to "meet the buyers" and have a five-minute presentation session with four buyers from four retailers:

Revy, Federated Coops, Lumberland, and Smith Barrager (a large west-coast distributor). Three weeks before the show I phoned the organizer and spoke to a wonderful woman. She explained that a booth would cost $1,200. I explained that VTC did not have that kind of money and offered her $600. She accepted, happy to get rid of the exhibition space at this late date. I asked if we could share the booth with another inventor, Jamie, who had a product to show; she agreed to this and also agreed that both Jamie and VTC would have separate meetings with the four buyers.

Before the show I frantically organized leaflets and samples. I bought a carpet for the 10-foot-square booth (it was cheaper than renting one), sent invitations out to retailers I thought would be attending the show, asking them to come to the booth to see the tools in action, and worried (of course) about what to wear. Since we planned to demonstrate how to use Caulk-Rite and needed to be comfortable, we decided on jeans and a casual shirt. Two identical short-sleeved shirts, sizes small and large, were required. It was late September so there were few summer clothes left in the stores, but I did manage to find two bright orange golf shirts in the correct sizes and had the words Caulk-Rite embroidered on them. These shirts were not expensive ($30 for the two), but they proved to be one of our best marketing tools. We have continued to wear them at trade shows over the years, and even though they are a little faded and splattered with silicone, in exhibition rooms full of men in dark suits they still make an impression.

The day before the show we furnished our half of the booth with a dining table from home and covered it with tools. Jamie used the other half to exhibit his invention, Cord-Lock, a device to hold electric cords together. We had the worst-looking booth at the show, but we were energized by the adrenaline flowing in the exhibition hall and by our own excitement. We met the buyers on the first day of the show and were amazed when each one committed to an order. In the space of 20 minutes we sold 5,000 Caulk-Rite tools and launched the business. If we had not taken part in the Western Hardware Show (which folded the following year), VTC would not have grown because I would not have been able to break down the resistance of the buyers and would have become totally disheartened.

The Caulk-Rite assembly party

We left the two-day Western Hardware Show elated that we had sold the 3,000 Caulk-Rite tools we had in our basement and an additional 2,000 we didn't have, but concerned that we needed to order another 20,000 tools. We tried to get a business loan to finance this big purchase, but failed. So instead we asked for money for a kitchen extension and succeeded. Banks are amazing creatures. Nine years after being turned down for a business loan, we are hounded weekly by these institutions—they all want to give us money for our business now. But when we really needed their help in the early days, they were nowhere to be found. Today the situation is no better for an inventor trying to fund a new product, and most end up turning to family and friends for financing.

Having ordered the plastic and rubber components, we next had to figure out how we were going to assemble and package 20,000 caulking tools. Because the two of us would never get this done on our own, we decided to hold a Caulk-Rite assembly party and invite our friends around for pizza, beer (both homemade—we still had little money), and some fun assembling tools. We invited 20 people and set up an assembly line in our living room/dining room one Saturday night. Two women showed up dressed to the nines, thinking it was a

"How to make sushi" party—they had obviously misheard Andrew's quietly delivered invitation. One neighbour and his date came after dinner at an expensive restaurant (it was the first time he had taken her out); he left at midnight and she stayed until 3 a.m., unwilling to break from the assembly line.

The party was a great success. Everyone pitched in and rotated tasks, some putting blades on tools, others putting tools into the packaging, and others boxing. And just when we thought we were done, Andrew would go to the basement and return with another box of tools and pour them noisily onto the table and floor. Every so often we stopped for beer and food, but there was always the pressure to carry on and not take too much of a break. We finally finished at 3 a.m., having packaged almost 10,000 tools.

I look back nostalgically at the Caulk-Rite assembly party and see it as one of the pivotal events of VTC. A year later, when we finally decided we could afford to pay someone else to assemble the tools, I was both relieved and a little sad to think there wouldn't be another party or another evening with just Andrew and me listening to CBC radio and assembling tools.

The efforts of our friends at the assembly party and our success at the Western Hardware Show meant that by the end of 1996 the Caulk-Rite tool was available in 50 Lumberland stores (now RONA) as well as about 40 Revy stores (now also RONA). And while VTC was growing and Andrew continued to work at UBC, I spent an increasing proportion of my time on caulking rather than criminology.

Our second trade show

In early 1997 we decided to take part in the Canadian National Hardware Show, an annual event in Toronto. This not only involved the cost of the booth for the three days ($2,000), but also the cost of booth fixtures and fittings, flights to Toronto, and hotel accommodation. We booked the cheapest available overnight flight and planned to save on transportation by staying within walking distance of the show at a somewhat seedy motel (for $50 a night instead of the $150 a night charged by the trade-show hotel). We arrived in Toronto at 7 a.m., bleary-eyed and sleep-deprived, and headed straight for a Home Depot outlet, where we expected to be able to purchase the materials necessary to furnish our booth. We had done our research in the Home Depots in B.C. and had assumed the same merchandise would be available in Ontario. This was not the case. The bright-yellow display plastic that we had planned to use for mounting the tools, so readily available in B.C. Home Depot stores, was nowhere to be seen. We had no choice but to purchase white Styrofoam ceiling tiles instead. We spent five hours at the exhibition hall, sticking Caulk-Rite tools to ceiling tiles. While all the other booths had fantastic graphics, photographs, and professional-looking displays using colour-coordinated products, we had the worst packaging in the world stuck on to ceiling tiles hanging on curtain rings. Even the booth next to us (selling, of all things, plastic drain pipe) had water cascading through black plastic cylinders, and bar stools and potted plants and little bowls of chocolates and candies—making it the sort of booth you *wanted* to visit, even if you could not get too excited about drain pipe. Our booth looked like it had been put together by a kindergarten class during an earthquake. We walked around the show after all our efforts, and you would have been hard-pressed to find two more tired and dejected people. We went to a pub near our motel to drown our sorrows, convinced we had just wasted close to $5,000. That night neither of us slept.

The next morning it was abundantly clear to anyone seeing us and our booth that we were green. We felt like total losers, standing in front of our feeble display with the sound of caulking tools clattering to the floor at regular intervals (they refused to stick to the ceiling tiles), wearing bright orange shirts and speaking with our out-of-place English accents. But we were unique in a way we had not anticipated—we demonstrated our product. In order to show how the Caulk-Rite tool worked, we applied a bad bead of caulk to a plastic T-bar and then used the Caulk-Rite tool to smooth it. In contrast, other exhibitors, many of whom were not the owners of their businesses, stood around in smart clothes and chattered or sat and read the newspaper. We developed a system whereby I would drag, sometimes literally, would-be purchasers into the booth as Andrew proceeded to demonstrate the Caulk-Rite tool. I would then follow up by taking names and orders. Although we were not supposed to do it, we sold tools at the booth and many vendors walked away with plastic bags holding between 5 and 55 tools (buy 10 get 1 free!). At the end of the day, exhausted, we sat on the floor of the exhibition hall and put more products together, my purse bulging with the cash we had taken, not yet daring to stop to discuss the day.

The booth across from ours was occupied by Canada's largest distributor of paint sundry items—Dynamic Paint Products. I had already asked this company to distribute Caulk-Rite, and although the owner had been interested initially, members of his sales force had not been enthusiastic. Consequently the owner decided not to list the Caulk-Rite tool, a decision we respected. But here we were—trade-show neighbours. During the first day he watched our booth and saw the interest we were generating. He saw crowds three deep and money changing hands. At the end of the second day we were sitting on the floor assembling Caulk-Rite tools and drinking pop when he came over to spend the next two hours on the floor with us (our booth did not have chairs), negotiating a contract, finalized by a handshake, that would give him the exclusive rights to sell Caulk-Rite in Canada. That night we completed an agreement (excluding the companies that had expressed interest or were already buying our product—Home Hardware, Revy, Lumberland, and Canadian Tire) that remains in effect today. Of course this buyer was very savvy and he demanded a price reduction. But flush with the response we had received at the show, we resisted giving him one. What we did do, though, was agree to engage a professional graphic design company to create new packaging that would facilitate rather than hinder sales. Although we would have done this eventually, the advice from this buyer who knew the market intimately moved us forward in a really vital way.

So in the end, the Canadian National Hardware Show was extremely good for Vancouver Tool. We worked harder than any other exhibitor. We talked and demonstrated more than any other exhibitor. We ran out of demonstration kits and spent much of the second night in our hotel bathroom drinking beer, eating takeout pizza and cleaning sticky caulk off the demonstration T-bars so they would be ready for reuse. We certainly had the most amateur-looking booth, but it did not seem to matter, as we found retailers and buyers loved new products and wanted to talk to the inventor. They wanted to determine how Andrew had come up with the idea, pick his brain about how it could be improved or modified, and give advice. During these conversations many retailers stressed the need for a caulk-removal tool, arguing that there was no such device on the market—and thus the seed of the Caulk-Away tool, our second product, was planted in the inventor's brain.

During the Toronto show I finally met the Home Hardware Big Buyer I had been unceremoniously chasing for almost six months. Over the course of the three-day show a lot of independent Home Hardware owners had asked if they could purchase Caulk-Rite through their central distribution warehouse, and I had to tell them I was still trying to persuade the buyer. I stressed to these dealers that they should tell the buyer to include Caulk-Rite in the range of products offered by Home Hardware. Dealers are not as scared of buyers as vendors are, and the ones I talked to at the show did a fine pestering job. On the final day of the show the Home Hardware Big Buyer showed up at our booth, complaining in a light-hearted manner about the number of dealers who were telling him what to do. He decided to list the tool, but not before he had negotiated discounts, rebates, delivery times, and so on. He also stipulated that VTC use Home Hardware Weathershield Caulk for any trade-show demonstration, something we still do today no matter where in the world we are exhibiting. I undertook all these negotiations, not really knowing what I was doing. Andrew just wanted to see his invention in the marketplace and would probably have given it away to accomplish this. What we would eventually come to understand was the importance of being firm about the price, which the buyer sees as the base for negotiating other deductions.

When we returned to Vancouver after the trade show, Andrew went back to work and I began coping with the mountain of business cards and hundreds of purchase orders and requests for samples and quotes. My first task was to divide these into three categories:

- "Hot leads"—the big boys I wanted to get back to immediately.
- "Response required"—the smaller retailers requiring samples or pricing information.
- "Thanks needed"—the individuals I wanted to remind about us and our product by thanking them for visiting our booth.

The Western Hardware Show and the Canadian National Hardware Show were two catalytic events for VTC. I advise any inventor to invest in relevant trade shows. They are extremely profitable for establishing leads and learning about business. So much can be gained from contact with fellow exhibitors and visitors to the show. Trade shows are exhausting and costly, but they are also rewarding, as long as you select the right one (see Chapter 5 for more detailed advice). The key for an inventor is to work the show from start to finish and to remember that no lead is too small to follow.

Initial marketing efforts

After the Canadian National Hardware Show I was still totally naïve about the conventions of marketing. I sent large bouquets of flowers to the two big (male) fish I had managed to net— Home Hardware and Dynamic Paint Products—as a way of saying thanks for believing in Caulk-Rite and VTC. I knew this would create a buzz in their offices and I wanted to get the VTC name out, but I still agonized over whether the $75 expenditure could be justified.

During the first year of VTC I spent most of my time sending out pricing information and samples. There were no huge sales at this time, but I still spent about six hours a day on marketing and trying to introduce Caulk-Rite to retailers. Although for the most part those who rejected the tool were quite polite ("No, we do not deal with one-SKU vendors," "It's too expensive," "Our customers don't need it," etc.), I still recall one awful phone call when I spoke to a buyer of a large retail chain based in Quebec. It was 8 a.m. I hadn't had a shower and was in my dressing gown—the joys of working from home. The buyer had received samples of the tool and I was asking whether he was interested in listing the product. He said, "Ms. Seagrave, I would *never* list your product."

"Why not?" I inquired with a shaking voice.

"Because the French is subservient to the English," he responded.

He was right. The French was slightly smaller because it takes more words in French than in English for the same instructions. His harsh words put me off selling to the Quebec market for the next four years.

While I was trying to deal with the polite and not-so-polite buyers, Andrew continued to work at UBC. During the summer of 1997 his time was increasingly taken up with office politics rather than architecture, and he began to suffer from headaches. As the summer progressed his work environment worsened, his headaches increased and so did his silences and moods. Finally I asked him to leave UBC, become a nice person again and invent the caulk-removal tool. It had been just over a year since we had started VTC and we had reached the stage where we could start to take money from the company—not a lot, but enough to pay the mortgage. In October 1997 Andrew left UBC and began to work on VTC's second product, Caulk-Away. The invention was finished that same month and VTC has been a full-time home-based occupation for both of us ever since.

Advice for the inventor

1. Talk and listen to the retailers who will be responsible for selling your invention. Seek their opinions and advice with humility. They are often right and have been making their living in this field for a number of years.

2. Make a list of the national companies or retailers you wish to approach and obtain the name, address, fax number, telephone number, and email address of each buyer. Use the same method to compile a list of smaller local retailers.

3. If you are a "one-SKU vendor" try to establish a good relationship with a reputable distributor to market your products. Be aware that this distributor will mark up your product by 30%, so set your price accordingly.

4. Attend and take part in trade shows whenever possible.

5. Demonstrate your product and show that it works. Be prepared to answer any questions.

6. Make cold calls to buyers whether you want to or not—no one likes doing this, but it is necessary. Always follow up and keep a precise account of what was said, by whom and when.

7. Send samples of your product (packaged *and* unpackaged) whenever possible.

8. Be firm on price and remember that the buyer sees this as a base from which a number of deductions can be taken.

CHAPTER 4: **Seeking Commitment from Buyers**

The Saleswoman and her Lovers

All relationships are difficult and none are more so than the one between the inventor of a new product (who wants so desperately to be loved) and the industry buyer (who never seems able to commit to a new relationship of any kind). Buyers are those mythical beings all vendors fear and worship. They are like long-lost lovers who have so much power (and know it) that they can make your heart race and skip a beat by saying "yes" to you and your product, or leave you dejected and emotionally bruised by saying "no."

One of our greatest advantages in launching VTC was my complete naïveté concerning the power of the buyer in the home improvement industry. It never crossed my mind that anyone would *not* want Andrew's fantastic little invention: he told me everyone needed one and showed me that the aisles of the largest home improvement stores were devoid of caulking tools. So with unbridled enthusiasm I launched into selling Andrew's invention. I brazenly called up buyers, sent Caulk-Rite samples, then phoned again and in my chatty manner asked straight out, "So why don't you have our tool in your stores?" I had no idea how much I had working against me. I was a woman. I had an English accent. And I had an untested product in bad packaging from a company no one had heard of. In my innocence I was managing to scratch at the hard hearts of buyers, but it was going to take a number of seductive moves before I could entice them into accepting all I and the tool had to offer.

When we first decided to sell Caulk-Rite we drew up a long list of companies, including Revy (now RONA), Lumberland (now RONA), RONA, Kent, Home Depot, Canadian Tire, Cloverdale Paint, General Paint, DH Howden, Cashway, Federated Coops, Home Hardware, and Group BMR. We devised a buyer contact sheet (see Appendix 1) for recording the name, address, telephone number, fax number, and email address of the buyer. We left space to describe the initial telephone call and any subsequent conversations, the messages left, and the result. And so I began keeping a detailed diary of my tumultuous love life.

Getting that first date

I learned early on that trade shows permit a form of "speed dating"—an opportunity to court and seduce buyers on a one-to-one basis. In the case of Canadian Tire, Revy, Home Hardware, Dynamic Paint Products, Federated Coops, DH Howden, and General Paint, this proved successful for us. What was surprising was how interest and commitment from one suitor (such as Home Hardware) would spark the same in others. Suddenly they all wanted to take us home to meet their mothers.

In establishing a relationship with the distributor, Dynamic Paint Products, we managed to get our tools in stores such as Wal-Mart, Sears, even Home Depot. In fact, I had been courting the Home Depot buyer for months, wanting to get something going with this big customer. He had received samples of both Caulk-Rite (in 1997) and Caulk-Away (in 1998) and had informed me he was not interested in either. Two weeks following his rejection of Caulk-Away (our second product, one he had asked specifically to be notified about), the tool received the Best New Product award at the Canadian National Hardware Show. One of the four judges was the president of Home Depot Canada, effectively the boss of the Home Depot buyer who had spurned my advances. I called the buyer and left a message saying I was disappointed he would not be listing the product, especially as his boss had thought it worthy of a prize. In other words, "You might not be prepared to offer me a date, but your older and better-looking brother is interested in me." A few weeks later we learned Home Depot was purchasing both Caulk-Rite and Caulk-Away through Dynamic Paint Products and in doing so was paying an additional 30% in distributor costs. We had won Home Depot's heart in a rather roundabout way.

Caulk-Away was named Best New Product at the 1998 Canadian National Hardware Show

Of course, some buyers opt for this additional cost because of the services included. Our distributor greatly facilitated sales to Home Depot by undertaking all merchandising (stocking shelves, consulting with buyers, offering discounts and promotions) and cross-merchandising (placing the tools in a number of different departments in Home Depot). Today both Caulk-Rite and Caulk-Away are "A" sellers (Home Depot designates products as "A," "B," "C," or "D" sellers based on sales), and they are on the permanent clip-strip program (hanging beside shelves or at the ends of aisles), which greatly facilitates sales.

Coping with courtship rituals

I quickly learned that having your tool listed with a large company does not mean that the company will then send a purchase order (a document describing the item required along with the quantity, price, delivery date, and location for shipping) and the relationship can begin. Oh no. There has to be some more seduction and flirting before the true courtship commences. It can take as long as 10 months from the time a buyer says "yes" to the time the product appears on store shelves. On very rare occasions it can take a mere four months.

Once the buyer has agreed, vendor contracts have to be negotiated and signed. These are lengthy documents (not unlike prenuptial agreements) that protect both sides and specify freight terms, return policies, boxing standards, and, of course, discounts. I have given up trying to understand the many discounts taken by the now quite small number of retailers we deal with, but they can include one or all of the following:

- An opening order discount for placing the initial order. ("It's our first date, so let's go Dutch.")

- Store-opening discount, requested when the retail chain opens new premises. ("This is an expensive place I am taking you to, so you need to help out with the bill.")
- Volume rebate for ordering a greater number of products. ("We have been dating for a long time and are both benefiting, so it's about time you paid for something.")
- Amalgamation discounts, requested when a hardware chain buys another hardware chain. ("We are running with a high-class crowd now, so you need to pay for yourself.")
- Product returned/damaged discount. ("Neither of us liked this place, so let's split the cost.")
- Early payment discount. ("You make more money than I do, so give me a break.")
- Advertising discount for placing the product in a catalogue or flyer. ("I need new clothes just to go out with you these days!")

Some discounts you have a choice about; others are mandatory.

I know of a case where new vendors priced their hardware product very competitively, not realizing that the price they had set would be whittled down so dramatically with all these discounts. VTC has not had to work within such tight margins because we offer a unique, patented product and we did not pitch the price too low initially. Inventors and small-business owners must remember that buyers *always* say the price is too high and that in time you will learn to tune these comments out.

Vancouver Tool Corporation has negotiated discounts with freight companies based on the volumes we ship so that we can price our goods FOB (free on board to their distribution centre), which means "delivered to the customer's warehouse." This saves buyers from having to figure out how much it costs to ship caulking tools from Vancouver to a warehouse in another part of the world. Once you have commitment from a buyer, you want to make the buyer's life as easy as possible, and pricing FOB is one way to do this. You never want to become a problem to buyers because they will not hesitate to make life difficult for you or terminate the relationship.

I have always found Canadian Tire a particularly fascinating company to court. For starters, it uses a system of "line reviews"—scheduled times when it looks at new products—so that even if a buyer meets you at a trade show and is interested in a relationship, nothing can happen until after the line review. Once you are in a relationship with "The Tire," you can't take anything for granted either. If you do not respond to an email from the company within 48 hours you can receive a $200 fine. And every year before Christmas the company reminds vendors not to send gifts to their buyers. Canadian Tire buyers change about every two years, so just when you think you are establishing good rapport with someone, that individual moves to purchasing power tools or gardening equipment and you have to start building a relationship with someone new. A vendor cannot deal with Canadian Tire without using EDI (electronic data interchange) for placing purchase orders, invoicing, sending shipment details, and so on. The Canadian Tire version of this system is supplied, ironically, by a company in the United States and costs us around $1,200 per year to access. Welcome to one more unanticipated business expense.

In yet another irony, I have found that the best place to meet a Canadian Tire buyer informally is not in Canada but at an international trade show. In 2004 we attended the International Hardware Show in Cologne, Germany, and had a booth in the Canadian section. About 10 Canadian Tire buyers visited the booth just, it would seem, to say hello to a fellow Canadian. One night after the show the Canadian Internet journal *Hardlines* hosted a party for the small group of Canadians in Cologne. There were not many of us, and all the Canadian Tire staff attended. I stood with one buyer drinking German beer and singing "O Canada" as the emcee played our anthem on his mouth organ—a good way to build vendor-buyer relationships (see Appendix 4).

Dating the unlikely suitor

Never write off a suitor just because he wears glasses or lives in the wrong part of town. One market that I did not at all anticipate when we started VTC has proved to be one of our most lucrative ones: the direct mail/TV/catalogue market. Any inventor needs to pay particular attention to this potential lover.

At the National Hardware Show in Toronto in 1998, a suited man came to our booth and asked whether he could have the exclusive rights to market our products through direct mail and catalogues in North America. By this point I had learned to be wary of some approaches. One of the disadvantages of trade shows is that you meet a number of overconfident idiots who say they can sell millions of your products. They tell you they regularly play golf with the CEO of Home Depot and have all the right contacts and then ask you to sign over the exclusive rights to market your product. So often such approaches come to nothing. In this case, I asked the man to contact me once I had returned to Vancouver, which he did. He sent me a list of catalogues I had never heard of and said he wanted to contact them. I signed the agreement, but assumed that because I had never purchased anything from a catalogue no one else did. I sent the contract back with a curt but polite "no discounts" message, expecting never to hear from the man again. I figured this was a relationship that was going nowhere.

But slowly and steadily Apollo Exports International started to submit larger and more regular orders, until in 2003 half our sales were through them.

Today I find working with Apollo International a delight. They always pay on time and, unlike many retail stores, do not expect all kinds of discounts. The moral of this story for the would-be inventor is to try the non-traditional catalogue market—date the unlikely suitor. Frequently products that conservative buyers are too fearful to list will get a big boost in a catalogue. Our best dollar sales to date have been for the Caulk-Doctor (see Chapter 6) on the QVC (Quality, Value and Convenience) home shopping network in the United States, primarily because the tools were unavailable in the retail outlets in that country. Apollo also increased our profile in the United States by successfully placing the tools in the *Skymall* magazine and in a number of direct-mail and Internet catalogues. Sales to this market are, however, short-term. Once the products are available in retail outlets, the premiums demanded by the catalogues can no longer be achieved and the item is dropped.

There are other unlikely suitors that the inventor should consider. One way VTC has managed to get products into the marketplace has been through private labeling. We have had Caulk-Rite and Caulk-Away tools produced in whatever colours and with whatever logos are required. Businesses that have taken us on in this way include a company in Quebec that sells bathroom surrounds. They found that many of their installed surrounds were unattractive because no one knew how to caulk properly. Now they include the Caulk-Rite tool in their installation kit. We also sell to StarBrite, a company that serves the marine industry internationally, and GE Silicones, a company that purchased our tools for a large promotion to Wal-Mart in the United States and RONA in Canada and sold them in conjunction with their sealants. These private-label orders are the easiest to deal with as the quantities are large and no packaging is required. And because VTC holds the patents, these customers can only access the tools through us.

Letting go of lost causes

The most overwhelmingly negative relationship experiences I have had involve the buyer who strings me along—says he is going to take me out but never does. I contact this kind of buyer a million times to arrange that long-promised date only to be given one of the following excuses:

- "I haven't had time to look at the sample."
- "I haven't received the sample so please send another."
- "I received the sample but one of my colleagues took it. Do you think you could send another one?"

Be wary of the buyer who is "always out" and never returns your telephone calls. And run the other way when you realize a buyer does not have the faintest idea what you are talking about. This happened to me recently when I spoke to a buyer from a very large organization in the United States. He said he had received the sample but hadn't tested it yet because he did not have any batteries (none of our tools *require* batteries).

Digging up dirt

One good way to learn about an individual buyer is to attend trade shows and speak to fellow exhibitors, many of whom have dated or tried to date the same buyer you are pursuing. This is when you can dig up the real dirt. You can find out whether your experience is unique, or whether other vendors have been kept waiting for meetings and have had their telephone calls ignored. You can also learn from fellow vendors which buyer you *really* want to get into bed with—the one who will treat you the way you want to be treated and shower you with big purchase orders.

In the early days of VTC I really appreciated buyers who were honest, such as the Home Hardware buyer who said truthfully that if his dealers wanted our product then he would order it. Or the Dynamic Paint buyer who told me truthfully that his sales force did not think the Caulk-Rite would sell. Then and now I have valued the buyer who *tells me the truth*. I like the buyer who tells me there is not a category review of the caulking-tool line for another eight months. I like the buyer who tells me that he thinks the packaging is awful. And I especially like the buyer who tells me he is not up to talking and will have to call later because his mother has just been diagnosed with a terminal illness or his pen has leaked on his pants or he spilled coffee all over the desk when he reached for the telephone.

Cultivating long-term relationships

In the early days we shipped small quantities of tools to any purchaser who wanted them. Now that we have succeeded in cultivating some healthy long-term relationships, we have a minimum-order requirement of 500 units and we effectively deal with only seven companies in Canada (Canadian Tire, Home Hardware, Sodisco-Howden, RONA, GE, Dynamic Paint Products, and Apollo International), three in the United States, and a further 10 internationally (in Sweden, Belgium, Spain, Poland, England, Germany, and Australia). There are tremendous benefits to this streamlining, including the reduction in paperwork and the increased opportunity for personal contact with each buyer.

Receiving a limited number of large cheques for thousands of dollars as opposed to lots of cheques for $50 is also a real bonus.

VTC was in business for seven years before we had our first bad debt. Dealing with the big boys who have credible reputations means payment is assured (even if it is not for the amount invoiced because of all the deductions taken). I have read that small businesses should never sell more than they can afford to lose. When we start to deal with a new customer I do not ask for credit references, believing the customer will only offer glowing ones anyway, but typically I have a casual conversation in which I stress that VTC is a small company that prides itself on delivering unique, patented products on time and will assist in whatever way possible in the marketing of these items. I say that in return we expect to receive payments on time. This personal contact and the reminder that the buyer is dealing with "Jayne and Andrew" helps. At the end of each year our accountant is amazed that we do not suffer from bad debts. If someone is late paying, I do make a telephone call and treat the issue light-heartedly while at the same time stressing that we operate a small business and will not ship when payments are outstanding. This practice seems to work. The one bad debt we have had came from a company in England that went bankrupt. We lost, but not a great deal, and we did as a consequence gain a Spanish customer who orders directly from us rather than through the bankrupt U.K. distributor.

The relationship between vendor and buyer should be a positive one that leads to profit for both. At the end of the day it should also be fun. To be successful selling a new product you must enjoy what you are doing. A couple of years ago one of our largest customers said to me at the close of a pretty tricky telephone conversation: "Jayne, if you ever need a job, promise you will come to me first." I found this to be a great compliment, especially as I felt this man and I had not always seen eye to eye. Another recent event at a trade show confirmed my perception that after many years VTC has been accepted into the hardware industry. We were not exhibiting at this particular event, but "walking the show," and I had agreed to see the Canadian Tire buyer in the exhibition hall. We met, discussed our tools and then spent the next 90 minutes having coffee and introducing each other to people we knew in the industry. Nine years ago I would have sold my mother for this kind of attention.

Advice for the inventor

1. Buyers will always say the price is too high. Make sure you leave room in your pricing to offer a discount. In getting a discount the buyer will feel he has won an important concession.
2. Expect negotiations with buyers to take a long time.
3. Make the buyer's job as easy as possible by pricing goods to include freight to their warehouse or warehouses.
4. Explore the direct mail/TV/catalogue market for your new product and expect to see a price much higher than you would in retail.
5. Be honest with a buyer and try to establish a personal rapport.
6. Be sure you respond to all the buyer's requests in a prompt and efficient manner.
7. Meet the buyer personally and during this meeting be prepared to demonstrate your product. This works best during trade shows, when buyers are prepared to visit the booths of would-be vendors and spend time discussing a product.
8. Find out about a particular buyer by spending time at trade shows talking to other vendors who know or sell to the buyer.
9. Humour and goodwill go a long way; send the buyer flowers.

CHAPTER 5: **Marketing the Invention**

How to Attract the Attention you Deserve

In speaking to hundreds of inventors over the last few years, I have learned that being a Great Inventor does not make you a Great Marketer. In fact, it is often just the opposite. Most inventors do not see and cannot understand the value of marketing. They do not want to invest in product packaging or presentation, nor do they believe any advertising (other than talking to a buyer) is needed. They see no value in something as "fluffy" as marketing and believe it is only for those who are introducing a different *colour* of mousetrap, not for those who have invented a *better* mousetrap. If Andrew had chosen another woman to spend his life with, there is a good chance he would never have succeeded with his invention: he needed a partner in life and in business who would understand that marketing is key to turning a good invention into a successful product.

I had no formal marketing training to begin with. My first degree is in sociology, and my second and third degrees are both in criminology. Luckily this did not stop me from learning about marketing in the ultra-conservative, old-fashioned home improvement industry, where my ideas for promotion were sometimes regarded as unusual. Over the last nine years I have devoted more time to marketing Vancouver Tool Corporation than doing anything else (aside from thinking about and looking after my children).

Promotional dos, don'ts and maybes

Marketing is pivotal to any business, especially one that is trying to sell a new product and has no track record. VTC has considered many different approaches and tried several, with varying degrees of success.

Two forms of promotion we have not used are print advertising and consumer shows. Advertising in magazines and newspapers tends to be expensive and does not often work for small operators. After some free coverage in trade magazines (*Hardware Merchandising*, for example), we have received inquiries, but the number of approaches has never been significant. And just as the expense of print advertising has made us cautious, so too has the expense of consumer shows. In addition, we have never liked the prospect of demonstrating our tools from 10 a.m. to 10 p.m. for as many as 10 days and laboriously selling each product for $5. It is far easier and ultimately more profitable to sell many thousands of tools to the buyer of a large retail chain at a trade show than to sell tools one by one to thousands of individuals at a consumer show. Nonetheless, I do know of inventors who have chosen to showcase their products at consumer shows after being worn down by rejection. There is a chance you will increase product awareness and therefore pressure buyers to list your invention, although I have rarely seen this happen in our industry.

A new small business with a limited sales and marketing budget cannot afford to gamble on expensive promotions that may not work. The chief forms of marketing we have used are trade shows, television advertising, creative delivery of samples, press releases, industry endorsements, and a web site.

Trade shows

Two trade shows provided a huge boost for VTC at the beginning (see Chapter 3). Since then, we have gone on to attend many of these events and have found them essential for getting our tools accepted in the marketplace (see Appendix 5 for a list of the shows we have attended). Based on our experience, trade shows are the most cost-effective way to market a new invention.

At the outset, the new business operator may question the amount of money and effort required to take part in these shows. And while you can be disappointed with the immediate results, you must remember that many of the effects are long-term ones. For instance, we recently received an order from a buyer in the United Kingdom who told me we had met over four years ago at a show. At that time he was working for another company and had been unable to get his bosses to list our caulking tools. Subsequently he changed companies and upon seeing VTC's products again succeeded in purchasing them. This illustrates the long-term power of the personal contacts that trade shows allow.

If you are going to attend trade shows you will need to begin by reading the trade literature and deciding which shows are relevant to you. Some shows have a "new vendor aisle" where booths are offered at a reduced rate (ideal for inventors who are strapped for cash). Over the last five years there has been a gradual decline in the number of shows. In the home improvement industry, questions are being asked about the survival of the Canadian National Hardware Show, and the International Hardware Show in Cologne now takes place every other year rather than every year. You will need to find out what is available for your particular product.

Once you decide on a trade show you will need to plan for your appearance there. You will want at least two people to staff your booth, as so often several visitors want different information at the same time. And if one of the Big Buyers arrives and wants to discuss your invention, you do not want to have to give the brush-off to the guy running a small general store in Manitoba who is interested in ordering five items. You will also need two people after the show: one to maintain the business and the other to follow up on all the leads generated at the show. I find it takes two to three weeks to fill the information requests received at a trade show and to respond to the email and telephone inquiries that come in later from individuals who have collected literature or samples at the show.

We order booth fixtures and fittings from the show organizers because we are now able and willing to pay the huge amount this convenience costs. We bring a suitcase full of tools (feeling lucky to have such a compact product) and furnish the booth with these and some enlarged photographs of the tools in retail outlets such as Home Depot to illustrate how successful they have been in Canada. When we first started attending trade shows we had a life-sized cardboard cut-out of James Dean with a Caulk-Rite tool in his hand (instead of a cigarette) and a bubble from his mouth that read "No caulk on my jeans." This was a tremendous draw to our booth. We now have laptop computers that run our corporate video demonstrating the tools.

Without a doubt there is a buzz of optimism surrounding the first day of a trade show. Many shows include a "new product showcase," which can help promote an inventor's ideas. Frequently this is the place buyers visit first upon arriving at a show. As I already mentioned, when we started we did not dress in smart power suits but wore blue or black jeans and shirts instead. On a Nike "Just Do It" shirt we sewed "Don't Just Do It, Do It Rite—Caulk-Rite," while on a "Gap Worldwide" shirt we embroidered "Fill the Gap Worldwide—Caulk-Injector." We have become somewhat more conservative recently. We now wear bright shirts with only the words Vancouver Tool Corp. Whatever you choose to wear, you need to be comfortable enough to stand in a very hot (and, in Europe, sometimes smoky) exhibition hall, talking and demonstrating for 10 hours.

I find trade shows exhausting because we answer questions incessantly, demonstrate non-stop, never sit down, never eat or drink enough and never have enough time to visit the

Do-It-Yourself
Show, London,
England

washrooms. We demonstrate both Caulk-Rite and Caulk-Away with T-bars—12-inch plastic strips that we fill with caulk and smooth into a perfect bead (over and over again).

After demonstrating we collect business cards from would-be buyers. Some are obviously not worth dealing with (a small retail shop in Greece that specializes in light fixtures would be one example), and these are filed away under a "no action" heading or thrown away. Some require a polite acknowledgement by letter, others require samples and specific pricing. Whatever action is required is written on the back of the business card, often with personal data such as "man with wife wearing a lot of gold" or "larger-than-life guy with purple hat and tattoo." These personal notes help me to visualize the individuals when I need to write to them. At the end of each day I organize these cards and make additional notes.

There are always quiet times during trade shows, especially on the last afternoon of the show and the final hour of each day. This is valuable time for the inventor, who can talk to other exhibitors and pick their brains about product development, suppliers, and the merits of various materials. Many exhibitors are sympathetic to new ideas, excited to speak to an inventor (or to anyone who will help pass the time) and generally want to help move an idea from the drawing board to the production line. As mentioned in Chapter 4, exhibitors are also a useful source of information on buyers and on dealing with the larger retail chains.

In addition to trade shows, the home improvement industry also has dealers' shows. These are essentially trade shows with restricted guest lists—only the retail outlets that are affiliated with the organizing show body are invited. For example, twice a year Home Hardware has a three-day dealers' market at its head office in St. Jacobs, Ontario, specifically for Home Hardware retailers. Here vendors are invited to showcase their products and speak directly to the dealers. It is a fantastic forum for the inventor of a new product who wants feedback from retailers. Canadian Tire, RONA, and Sodisco-Howden also invite vendors to take part in these kinds of forums (we have never been invited to the Canadian Tire or RONA one). We have attended the Home Hardware dealers' market on a number of occasions and found it to be one of the busiest and best environments for getting our new items promoted. It is also a lot of fun.

Television advertising

In January 1999 we spent $10,000 (including production and air time) for a 30-second TV commercial to follow a special promotion on the renovation industry that was being aired by a TV station in British Columbia. At the time this was a very significant sum of money for us. We attended the first meeting for this when our son Jack was just nine days old, so I spent the morning learning about TV commercials and breast feeding. It was definitely worth the inconvenience. The money we spent increased our profile with consumers and with our buyers. I was able to call my buyers and inform them we were running a four-week advertising campaign. I could stress the need to stock their shelves with more products and perhaps think of putting us at the end of an isle or with an "As seen on TV" sign. Revy stores did this.

Ten thousand dollars is a lot for a small business, but in the long run it was money well spent. Home Hardware and Revy suddenly saw us as a company here to stay. Canadian Tire insisted that it appear first on the closing "Available at …" frame. A few years later we repeated the same commercial on the specialty Home and Garden TV network in Canada and then later undertook advertisements for our new grouting tools in the same way. As before, we notified our buyers about the campaign and prepared them for increased consumer interest.

Creative delivery of samples

When launching a new product or tool today, I always send at least two packaged samples and one unpackaged sample along with a covering letter (see Appendix 2) and product information sheet (see Appendix 3). Initially it did not cost a lot to produce and send out Caulk-Rite samples—one of the great things about Andrew's invention. Retailers love new items and if they are the first to try out an item they can become very excited about it. Now that we have moved to selling more kits and have developed a range of professional-quality steel tools, sending out samples has become increasingly expensive. The items we ship now weigh and measure more and require more costly packaging and postage, especially to Europe. Still, we know that distributing samples is a crucial part of the sales and marketing process. Many inventors, who want to send out samples only once they believe a sale is guaranteed, must accept the fact that there is no guarantee and that it costs money (and time) to introduce a new product. And the only way the inventor is ever going to fully recoup these costs is by getting the product to the marketplace.

I learned early on that if I wanted to compete with the big boys (such as Stanley Tools and GE Silicones) and their marketing teams, I needed to think of innovative ways to get "that pathetic little plastic tool" into the mind, the hand, and the heart of the buyer. Frequently the product sample is opened by an assistant or secretary and becomes separated from the covering letter and product information sheet, as buyers—perhaps because they tend to be male—often operate in chaotic environments. To ensure that the buyer and not his or her sidekick has the pleasure of seeing your raison d'etre, you must package and deliver your samples in a creative way. For example, a few years ago I packaged one of our new products in red tissue paper and sprinkled this wrapping with thousands of pieces of confetti. When the buyer unwrapped the tool, this confetti cascaded onto his desk and suit. I had done this to hint, perhaps too subtly, at the prospect of a perfect marriage between the buyer and our tools. I soon learned from the buyer that the janitors at his office were refusing to clean his area because of all the confetti. I relished the idea that each day he would enter his office, see the confetti on his floor and think of me and VTC products. In addition, his colleagues would undoubtedly visit him and ask why his office was covered in confetti, and then find out about the unconventional delivery of a new VTC product.

When we launched our second product, the Caulk-Away caulk-removal tool, I sent "birth announcements" (which four buyers have subsequently told me they thought really creative). I purchased traditional-looking cards from a stationery store and wrote that VTC was pleased to announce the birth of its second child, named Caulk-Away: "The proud parents are delighted with the 4½-inch red tool weighing 4 grams; a much-wanted sibling for Caulk-Rite."

Last year I found shoelaces with I ♥ VANCOUVER on them. I added the word TOOL to read I ♥ VANCOUVER TOOL and sent them in shiny black jewellery boxes to all my buyers. Three of the 12 buyers I sent them to emailed to say thanks. I have also sewn the Caulk-Rite tool onto the hands of stuffed teddy bears and moose purchased for around $3 each. I know these now reside not only on the desks of my buyers but also on the desks of people in sales and accounts (where they keep VTC on the minds of the important individuals who pay the invoices). At Christmastime, I once dressed Andrew in a rented Santa Claus outfit and took photographs of him repairing bathroom grout for our "Seasonal Groutings" card. Another time we sent "Merry Caulkmas" cards to suppliers and buyers.

Caution is advised, however, when it comes to innovative delivery methods. Just after September 11, 2001, I sent a brightly coloured package with no return address to Canadian Tire. When it got to the mailroom, staff called the police to investigate, worried the package might explode. In that instance I received a curt but polite note from the buyer asking me to make sure all future correspondence exhibited a return address. This I now do (you never want to upset Canadian Tire).

Throughout the year I use lots of cards—for Christmas, Easter, Canada Day, Halloween, and Valentine's Day. As well as sending cards to buyers employed by companies that purchase VTC products, I send cards to other support staff employed by the company. When we receive an initial order, no matter how small, I always send a thank-you card. If the customer is not in North America, I ensure there is some Canadian content—stickers of Mounties, beavers, and lumberjacks on the envelope, colourful Canadian stamps, and maple-leaf wrapping paper. My thank-you cards serve two purposes. First, these cards let companies know we are grateful for their business and conscious they are taking a risk listing a new product. Second, they encourage companies to pay on time. I believe people at any company have a harder time not paying an invoice if they have received a pretty card or a cuddly bear from the organization they owe money to.

Press releases

I always write and distribute press releases when we launch a new product or do something newsworthy. For example, I sent out press releases when Caulk-Away received the Best New Product award at the Canadian National Hardware Show, when we got the Exporter of the Month award from Industry Canada, and when we took part in an international trade show in Europe. Hundreds of marketing books describe how to write a press release and I have no intention of adding to this literature by explaining the process (see Appendix 4). If you are not confident enough to author your own press release you can always hire a marketing firm. But whatever you do, make sure you send press releases of some kind. Because of press releases VTC has been featured in the *Vancouver Sun*, *B.C. Business*, *Business in Vancouver*, *Vancouver Magazine*, *Canadian Business*, the *National Post*, *Reader's Digest*, and a number of European and American publications. All this publicity has been free of charge and has assisted considerably in raising our corporate profile.

I do have to say that there is no discernible logic to the way one article based on a press release can spawn others. The article in the glossy business magazine that you think will be picked up by other outlets is ignored, while the article in the local free newspaper receives attention everywhere. A few years ago we were featured in a *B.C. Business* article that few people seemed to read (based on the few telephone calls and emails we received following publication). But this article eventually prompted a U.S. magazine, *The Entrepreneur*, to carry a bigger article on VTC in both its U.S. and Canadian editions. This in turn led to VTC being featured on the America On-Line (AOL) pages on two separate occasions. At about the same time, a friend who is a freelance journalist submitted an article to *Reader's Digest Canada* about inventors and included a funny photograph of Andrew and me in the shower with our caulking tools. As a result of these articles the American Home Business Association sent a production crew to spend a day with us so we would be featured on an infomercial to promote that agency.

Subsequently they also interviewed us for a magazine article. All of this shows that you never know where a particular piece of promotion can lead. While you might think no one reads a certain magazine just because you don't, this is not necessarily the case.

Industry endorsements

The home improvement industry has seen a burgeoning of how-to shows on radio and television, as well as a surge in newspaper and magazine articles and even entire publications devoted to home renovation. Our caulking and grouting tools have received endorsements from a number of home improvement experts who are featured in various shows and publications. If these endorsements occur before the products are in the stores, it can lead to consumer frustration, as was the case in the United States when Caulk-Rite was reviewed in over 200 newspapers one weekend (an article in the *Philadelphia Enquirer* newspaper was syndicated widely) and yet no one could purchase the tool. While occasionally I am asked to pay for these recommendations, I have never done so. We have provided free samples for give-aways at home shows attended by these industry experts. We did, however, have to stop sending free samples to one such expert after we found the tools were appearing on his web site for purchase, but that is another story.

Web sites

Everyone needs a web site these days—it is an effective and relatively inexpensive way to advertise. Our Vancouver Tool Corporation site (www.vancouvertool.com) is primarily for making contact with buyers and potential international customers. It contains demonstrations of the tools in action and contact information. We do not sell tools from this site. Our policy has always been to sell large numbers of products to a small number of reputable players. We have never explored the option for credit-card payments on the web. Instead, our products are available for sale on the Internet through companies such as QVC (www.qvc.com), *Skymall* magazine, and various catalogues (www.improvementscatalog.com, for example) and shopping networks.

In addition to the traditional marketing concepts described here, we have been interviewed on local TV and radio programs and spoken to groups at academic institutions and meetings of the B.C. Inventors Society. Two years ago we took part in a "Women Only" renovation night at the local RONA store. These events are not cost-effective if judged by the number of sales achieved, but they are good ways to promote the name of your business. Five years after we started the business, I met a woman on a beach in Hawaii who asked me what I did in Vancouver. I was thrilled when she responded, "Hey, I know that tool. I've got one!" A few weeks after this I was driving back from the United States when the Canada Customs official wanted to know the nature of my business. I told him and he said, "Proceed, I've seen you guys on TV." Five years may seem like a long time to wait for these kinds of reactions (especially when it feels like you have worked every minute of every day to market your tools), but it is all worthwhile when strangers you meet on foreign shores know about your invention.

Advice for the inventor

1. Critically assess whether you are the right person to market your product. If you are not, carefully consider employing someone to do it for you.
2. Avoid print advertising, which is costly and does not appear to deliver results in terms of sales. Similarly, think twice before participating in expensive, labour-intensive consumer shows.
3. Consider attending trade shows. Find out which shows are best for your product, plan for your appearance, and be prepared to follow up on contacts made. If possible, start small and start local.
4. Consider TV advertising as a way to promote your company as well as a way to sell your product. Only undertake TV advertising once your product is available in stores.
5. Send at least two samples whenever possible and always follow up to ensure the buyer has received them and is considering the products.
6. Think of innovative ways to deliver samples to buyers and to remind buyers about your products.
7. Use press releases—a free form of promotion—whenever possible.
8. Obtain endorsements if this is appropriate for your product.
9. Establish an Internet presence with a web site of some kind. If possible, use videos to demonstrate your invention.
10. Start small and locally at first.

A "One-SKU Vendor" No More

After experiencing some success with our first product, we knew we had to expand and become more than a one-product vendor. Our progress in this regard can be seen in the following table.

VTC Expansion

Year	Product introduced
1996	Caulk-Rite
1998	Caulk-Away
1999	Caulk-Injector
1999	Caulk-Kit
2001	Caulk-Doctor
2002	Grout-In
2002	Grout-Out
2003	Grout-Doctor
2004	Caulk-Rite-Pro
2004	Caulk-Away-Pro

Today we hold patents on five tools (Caulk-Rite, Caulk-Away, Caulk-Injector, Grout-In, and Grout-Out). Although we are clearly no longer a one-product vendor, Caulk-Rite continues to be our most successful item based on the numbers sold, even though Caulk-Doctor produced more dollars in sales in 2002 and 2003.

Rolling out these different products has taught us that the development and introduction of inventions is a costly and time-consuming process. We undertook this primarily to grow Vancouver Tool Corporation, but it has also kept us stimulated. We do not want to do the same thing day after day. VTC has a reputation as a company with innovative products. Recently one of our buyers said that there are very few totally new items available, especially ones that work, and that VTC is known as one of the few companies that consistently "delivers something different." We learned a lot from the development of our products, and I think the story of each product has something to teach inventors who want to produce and market an invention.

Caulk-Rite

Once the Caulk-Rite patent was in place Andrew approached three large manufacturing companies and asked whether they were interested in considering Caulk-Rite for their product lines. All responded positively. The first manufacturer was U.K.-based Plasplugs, which had a number of products for the tiling/caulking market. We sent a covering letter, photographs, and a description of the Caulk-Rite tool and received a quick rejection—it turned out the company was already exploring a similar product. Plasplugs now markets a caulk-application tool that is based on different (and less effective) technology than ours.

The second large manufacturer we approached was 3M, which markets a wide range of plastic tools in the United

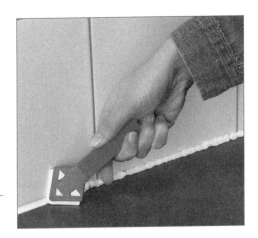

The Caulk-Rite tool
that started it all

States. They responded with a form letter saying they were not interested (the sort of discouraging letter I suspect many inventors have become all too familiar with).

The final manufacturer we approached was Richards Tools, a Quebec-based Canadian company that markets a range of tools for the tiling market. They wrote back to say they were "thinking about it." Andrew called them on a number of occasions to determine how these deliberations were going and they were always still "thinking about it." After we had been in business for four years, we finally had a meeting with the president of Richards Tools. He expressed interest in the exclusive rights to market our products but it was too late. By that time our tools were in every large home improvement retailer in Canada and the president was forced to admit (to his chagrin and our satisfaction) that Richards Tools had made a mistake in not listing Caulk-Rite.

In all our conversations with inventors, we have never met anyone who has successfully managed to sell an invention to a large manufacturer. Large corporations are conservative and do not want to take risks with unproven items. Just as buyers are reluctant to list new products, those responsible for new product development are unwilling to take chances. Inventors have frequently asked us how they can access the finances necessary to bring their invention to production and we have had to say that it always seems to come down to the inventor finding the finances to fund the invention process.

Today the Caulk-Rite tool remains our most successful product and we continue to produce it in many different colours, market it in many different ways and ship it all over the globe. We have probably sold about five million Caulk-Rite tools. We sell packaged Caulk-Rite tools to customers in Canada, and for all other jurisdictions we ship the tools in bulk for packaging in whatever language is required. The rules of bar codes, recycling, and packaging vary considerably from jurisdiction to jurisdiction (for example, home improvement retailers in the U.K. have much less space to display goods than big box retailers in North America do, so they demand more compact packages and English-only instructions). Recently we developed small "hanging cards" that we supply free of charge along with a fastener for bulk orders of Caulk-Rite and Caulk-Away. This allows international customers to apply their own label to the cards and has proved to be a great marketing tactic as it eases many of the packaging headaches international customers face.

The Caulk-Rite tool is made from recycled plastic, and the only modification to the original tool of almost 10 years ago is the blade, which is now made through the injection molding process. When we started, the blades were cut from a long thin ribbon of rubber, which varied slightly in thickness and ended up being very difficult to insert into the tool handle. Two injection molding companies are now used for the production of Caulk-Rite and we have two-, four- and eight-cavity molds. These molds have removable inserts so that we can easily take out the Caulk-Rite name and leave the tool blank, or add another company's logo. All tools state they are made in Canada and have the patent numbers for Europe, Canada, and the United States on them. This allows us to easily identify any counterfeit tool.

Caulk-Away

The prototyping and production of our second product, Caulk-Away, was undoubtedly a smoother process because we had the experience of developing Caulk-Rite. We formally introduced the Caulk-Away tool at the 1998 Canadian National Hardware Show. We sent samples to buyers a few weeks before the show and a letter inviting them to a demonstration of the tool at our booth. It was fantastic to move beyond the one-product vendor label, and although Andrew did not believe the tool to be as good as Caulk-Rite (and subsequent sales have proved this to be the case—for every 10 Caulk-Rite tools we sell 7 Caulk-Away tools), this was not the reaction of the industry, which gave it the Best New Product award. This award and the accompanying Oscar-like trophy (which fell apart upon receipt—how fitting that the organizers of a renovation show would have trouble gluing something together) gave us and Vancouver Tool a fantastic lift. That night we celebrated in the Wheatsheaf on Queen Street in Toronto, one of the oldest pubs in the city. We stood the trophy proudly on our table, inviting comments from other patrons, many of whom received free tools so they could share in our success.

Caulk-Away is now produced by two injection molding companies in British Columbia. Unlike Caulk-Rite, which is made from the cheapest recycled plastic material, Caulk-Away is produced from the strongest plastic available to make it durable and keep it from developing rough edges that scratch tile or enamel.

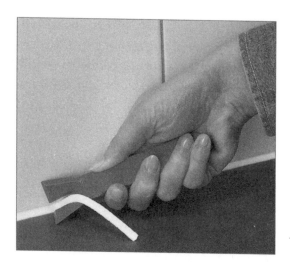

Caulk-Away tool

One of the biggest surprises to me was how quickly buyers accepted Caulk-Away. I subsequently realized that it is relatively easy for buyers to list another product from a company they already deal with—they do not need to set up a complicated vendor agreement and they feel secure dealing with a company that has a proven track record. This perhaps explains why so many products that may be deemed superfluous to requirements are available in hardware stores.

Naming Caulk-Away proved to be entertaining. We had wanted to call it Caulk-Gone or Caulk-Out, but our graphic designers pointed out that guys on building sites would collapse with laughter every time one called to another, "Hey Buddy, where's your Caulk-Gone?" or "Have you got your Caulk-Out?"

Today we produce Caulk-Away in bulk for sales internationally, just as we do Caulk-Rite, and we can add different names to the tool. While Caulk-Away is not as popular as Caulk-Rite (more people need to apply caulk than remove it), it is still our second-best-selling item and a key component to our success. Caulk-Away wholesales and retails for the same price as Caulk-Rite. Although Caulk-Rite has two components and requires assembly, it is made from cheap plastic. In contrast, Caulk-Away is produced from a more expensive, more durable plastic. Production costs are therefore similar. We have not increased the prices of the tools to buyers since we launched them. Caulk-Away carries a full patent and of course is trademarked.

Caulk-Injector and Caulk-Kit

In 1999 we introduced two new products. The first, Caulk-Injector, was invented to address the problem of applying silicone or caulk when deep penetration is required—for example, if you have a large crack in a driveway or swimming pool. The Caulk-Injector permits far deeper applications than conventional processes because of its two components: one for in-corner crevices and one for flat-surface cracks. There was no need to invent another caulking gun, as these are being manufactured in their billions offshore at prices we could not match. Increasingly the "squeezy" no-gun-required tubes of caulk are being sold, suggesting that sealant applied by a caulking gun may soon become obsolete.

Caulk-Injector tool

We had problems with the Caulk-Injector tools from the outset. First we had trouble getting the rubber pad to stick to the plastic tool. We solved this by applying stronger (and more expensive) glue. Then the hinged sections kept breaking. When we received the first large order from the injection molders I picked up a tool and watched it fall apart in my hands. We had produced 20,000 worthless plastic objects. Unfortunately, we

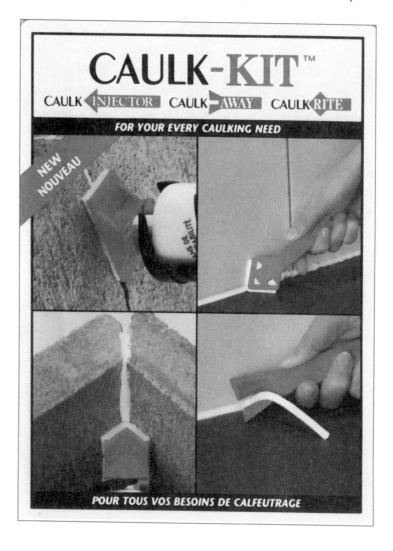

had already sent out samples by this point so I had to contact the buyers and ask them not to test the tools and to expect replacements soon. While I found this very embarrassing, it did give me the opportunity to contact buyers again and ensure they remembered my name. What surprised me was the casual way buyers accepted this failing. Many new products have teething problems and the buyers saw what had happened as quite natural. Several buyers recounted horror stories about products from companies far larger than VTC.

At the same time we launched Caulk-Injector we also launched a kit containing Caulk-Rite, Caulk-Away, and Caulk-Injector tools—the Caulk-Kit. Most buyers took both products but it soon became apparent that the Caulk-Injector was not selling and Caulk-Kit sales were slow. In late 2000 we discontinued Caulk-Injector as a separate product. Obviously it was too specialized an item. Sales of Caulk-Kit, however, were growing steadily and we were receiving repeat orders. We unpackaged the 18,000 Caulk-Injector tools we had and repackaged them in Caulk-Kits, giving anyone with more specialized requirements all the tools they would need.

Caulk-Doctor

In March 2001 I visited friends and home improvement stores in England. (I sometimes wonder whether there will ever be a time in my life when I am not drawn to visit do-it-yourself emporiums.) While walking down the sealant-tool aisles I was again reminded of just how confusing the merchandise can be. So many sealants, for so many tasks, with so many promises and so many instructions! At the same time I had just read that 25% of women in North America live by themselves. I considered the fact that these women must often be faced with mildew-infested, poorly applied silicone in their bathrooms and kitchens and feel unable to tackle the problem. It seemed you would need a Ph.D. just to figure out what sealant you needed to start with. At that moment I envisioned another VTC kit consisting of a Caulk-Rite caulk-application tool, a Caulk-Away caulk-removal tool, a squeezy tube of GE Kitchen and Bath Silicone (no caulking gun required), protective nitrile gloves (good for people with latex allergies) to keep silicone from coming into contact with the skin, wipes to clean any mess, and a clearly written instruction leaflet.

At first I wanted to name the product Reno-Woman and pitch it directly to the female market. Although I still believe there is considerable potential for this idea, I also think we did the right thing by settling on a less limiting name—Caulk-Doctor—especially as we could buy blue nitrile gloves to reinforce the "doctor" idea.

I spent the next six months designing the kit. Unlike our other products, this was not a new invention but a new way of marketing two existing tools. Our graphic designers developed a great logo of a doctor with caulking tools in his pockets, and we purchased wipes from a company in the U.S.—our first import. I knew the wonderful Canadian sales representative for GE Silicones because GE had ordered product from us and we had worked close to each other at trade shows. GE has an excellent reputation, so we decided to include its Kitchen and Bath Silicone in the Caulk-Doctor kits. While we could have found significantly cheaper sealants, I liked the liaison with GE. I had considered they might not want to package their sealants with our tools, but they were delighted at the prospect of receiving free TV advertising in addition to gaining the sales.

I had thought that Caulk-Doctor would sell well in catalogues and through the home-shopping channels. What I had not anticipated was just how successful this would be. In 2003 VTC purchased more 14-ounce tubes of Kitchen and

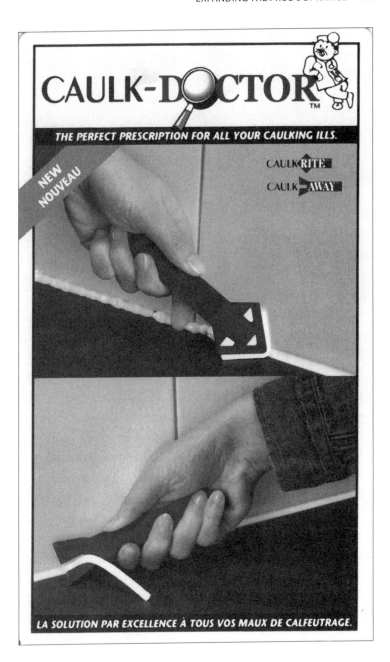

Bath Silicone from GE than Home Depot Canada did. At one point 7,000 Caulk-Doctor kits were sold in a 10-minute period on the QVC (Quality, Value and Convenience) shopping channel. In fact, half of VTC's dollar sales in 2003 were earned by Caulk-Doctors sold through the QVC network in the U.S. We sold the Caulk-Doctor kits through our distributors in Toronto, who went on air to demonstrate the product and showed viewers it really worked.

While the Caulk-Doctor sold well on the QVC network in the U.S., it did not do so well in retail outlets in Canada. This is understandable, given that consumers visiting retail outlets already carrying Caulk-Rite, Caulk-Away, and an array of silicones could quickly figure out that it was cheaper to purchase the items separately than to buy the Caulk-Doctor kit. Also, many stores in Canada, especially the smaller ones such as Home Hardware, offer good personal assistance to anyone totally confused about applying caulk.

One of the largest problems we had with the Caulk-Doctor turned out to be the supply of GE Silicone. GE is undoubtedly the biggest company we deal with. Before developing the Caulk-Doctor, we had depended exclusively on B.C. suppliers, with whom we had excellent relations. I had naïvely assumed that big organizations with large staffs could deliver the correct product on time. This was not the case. Our biggest headaches in the entire history of VTC involved non-shipments, the shipment of 20,000 tubes of silicone in the wrong packaging (red rather than the blue ordered), faulty packaging (leaky and mislabelled tubes), late delivery, and incorrect customs brokerage information, which meant we could see the pallet of product we so desperately needed at the UPS customs warehouse at Vancouver Airport but did not have the paperwork to access it. All these issues were unanticipated and unpredictable, and for two weeks when we had orders to fill and deadlines to meet I would wake at 2 a.m. and worry about silicone.

This was a bad time. I have always been a well-organized person and prided myself on fulfilling my commitments. Having to depend on other suppliers meant I was not in control. Over time these issues were resolved. To be fair, our contacts at GE did work hard to try to correct mistakes. They did return our frantic hourly telephone calls, worked late into the night and sent product to our customers at considerable expense to themselves (silicone is not light and costs a lot to ship by air). While we made money on the Caulk-Doctor it was not without considerable stress, which led me to question whether we as a company might be growing too quickly.

Caulk-Rite-Pro and Caulk-Away-Pro

In 2004 VTC built on the strength of Andrew's original inventions and introduced Caulk-Rite-Pro and Caulk-Away-Pro. This involved taking the Caulk-Rite and Caulk-Away designs and producing them in metal with replacement blades for the professional/contractor market. When Andrew had first thought of Caulk-Rite, he had wanted to produce it in steel for the contractor market, but he soon realized this would be too expensive.

Caulk-Away-Pro
 and
Caulk-Rite-Pro

So far the reaction to the professional-quality tools has been positive, especially in Europe. However, we are still in the early days with these tools and will need to see what happens before pursuing more of this kind of product.

Grout-In and Grout-Out

In 2002 VTC went beyond caulking and introduced two new products. Grout-In is a plastic tool for applying and cleaning tile grout. It retails for under $5 and has two blades, one for the grout application and one for the grout clean-up. There have been no real problems with Grout-In (other than the lack of sales, which is a big problem of a different kind).

Grout-Out is a far more complicated matter. It has metal components as well as plastic ones and attaches to the end of an electric drill to erode unsightly tile grout. Andrew spent a lot of time with steel manufacturers discussing the correct metals to use and benefiting from the expertise of one local steel-working company. While an earlier version of Grout-Out was fine for small tasks, when the tool was used for extensive periods the plastic casing containing the blades would heat up and melt. We solved this problem by devising a new (and more expensive) casing.

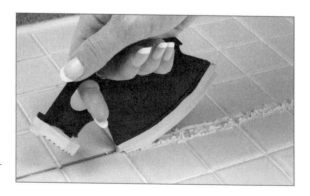

Grout-In tool

Grout-Out tool

Our next problem was equally perturbing and completely unrelated to production. I had assumed that the same buyers who ordered our caulking tools would order our grouting tools, but this was not the case. In the home improvement industry grouting tools are not considered paint sundry items, they are tiling items. I had to start afresh with a whole new set of buyers. Our main Canadian distributor, Dynamic Paint Products, did list the grouting tools but returned them after a year, saying they had had little success with them because their buyers were not responsible for this line. Home Hardware has included the tools, and they are still under review at Canadian Tire.

At the same time we developed Grout-In and Grout-Out we put together a Grout-Doctor, assuming that since Caulk-Doctor had sold well so would Grout-Doctor. It did not. It bombed completely, leaving us to write off a large number of blue tools and tubes of grout.

In considering our relative lack of success with the grouting tools, I've come to a few conclusions:

- Fewer people apply grout than apply caulk so the market for grouting tools is smaller.

- When you move into a new area you have to establish relationships with a different set of buyers, and this takes time. Once again you are a "One-SKU Vendor" with no track record.
- When a market is new to you (and smaller), you need to spend time exploring possibilities. When we were first marketing the grouting tools, we were still spending a lot of time serving our caulking-tool customers and may not have done as much research as we should have.
- To sell something you have to believe in it fully. I was reluctant to promote Grout-Out because I was aware of its design flaws and may not have done as good a job as I could have.

We recently started to sell Grout-In to a company that is having some success selling it in the craft retail sector—again, a consumer I had not anticipated. Although sales are not buoyant, I am not prepared to write off the grouting tools just yet and neither is Andrew. Today he believes the patent for Grout-Out is the best of the five he holds.

Advice for the inventor

1. Start with production runs that are as small as possible to avoid unnecessary expenses. We started with a one-cavity mold, then moved to using two-, four- and eight-cavity molds when we could afford them.

2. Be sure your product carries your patent numbers or the words "patent pending."

3. When introducing another product, approach a buyer you are already dealing with.

4. Try to build a family of products and present these to one buyer with whom you have established a rapport. Build on your successes and try not to cross buying lines.

5. Seek advice from as many different people as possible when you name your product.

6. Think of different ways your invention can be marketed to facilitate sales. You might want to consider packaging it with other products, as we did with the Caulk-Injector.

7. Obtain written agreements from your suppliers that specify delivery times. Consider imposing financial penalties if suppliers fail to deliver on time.

8. When possible, have back-up suppliers in case there are problems with the selected supplier.

9. Seek to piggy-back with others who already have a presence in the market. GE is a much better-known company than VTC and has facilitated the introduction of our tools to the North American market.

CHAPTER 7: **New Market Development**

Sleeping (Or Not) with the Elephant

Our international sales efforts have been conducted in a generally uncoordinated manner. We know we need to get products to other marketplaces in order to protect our patents and grow the business, but we have not drafted a formal business plan for the two markets we have chosen to enter—the United States and Europe. It has been clear from the beginning that we are unlikely to take our products to certain jurisdictions: China, Russia, India, Africa, and the Middle East. Aside from the fact that people in these regions do not use sealants to any great extent, we feel many of the approaches from these regions have not been bona fide.

After nine years in business I cannot say yet whether we have been successful in our international marketing. We have experienced many frustrations and few rewards in our attempts to market the tools to both the United States and Europe.

Selling to the United States

Our caulking tools sell *so* well in Canada. There is not a single large Canadian home improvement retailer that does not carry our caulking tools. While sales grow in Canada year by year (at a rate of 30%), our tools remain largely unavailable in the United States. It is my greatest frustration. The population of Canada is 36 million; the population of America is 10 times greater. The potential market remains huge and yet to date has not been accessed. Each week we receive approximately 30 emails from individuals in the U.S. who wish to purchase our caulking tools, and I direct them to the extensive list of catalogue companies and TV shopping networks (where these people have usually seen the products but are looking for the more reasonably priced retail alternative). In analyzing the situation, I am unsure whether we have been unable to crack the U.S. nut because of the unique American culture, which is so different from Canadian culture, or because of our decision to commission distributors who have little interest in promoting the products.

Within the first year of launching Caulk-Rite, we started to explore the U.S. market. As trade shows had proven to be so successful for us in Canada, we tried a number in the United States. Without exception U.S. buyers appreciated the tools, but they insisted that we secure distribution in the U.S. No one wanted to purchase from a Canadian company, especially a "one-product vendor," no matter how sexy the little caulking tool was.

During the trade shows we exhibited in south of the border (see Appendix 5), we were regularly approached by manufacturers' agents who were willing to list the product and who promised us the world in sales terms. These agents act a little like distributors but really they only secure the sale—they do not deal with the logistics of shipping, payment, purchase orders, discounts, and all the other issues our Canadian distributors care about. Sales agents make the pitch to a buyer, and if the buyer accepts the product the agent is paid a commission. I had attended an Industry Canada seminar where we were advised that if a business was going to use manufacturers' agents, it should treat them as employees and spend time selecting the right ones. Industry Canada suggested that the agents you need are *not* the ones who are looking for work. I took this to be good advice. At trade shows we were approached by a number of larger-than-life individuals who tended to be suited men promising they were best friends with/went to school with/had married the sister of/lived next door to the senior Home Depot buyer and therefore could get our caulking tools in all Home Depot stores within a month. However, when we went beyond the surface bluster and asked these representatives for references or details of similar products in their portfolios, we received nothing. The Industry Canada seminar estimated that good manufacturers' agents would take six months to recruit, and the best would be reluctant to include a new item from another country in their inventory.

Manufacturers' agents are used extensively in the United States, but we decided not to go this route, which I found too confusing, difficult if not impossible to administer, and fraught with problems. Not only do these agents work only certain territories or states, they also require exclusive agreements. There then appears to be little control or accountability. How do you know these manufacturers' agents are actually selling your products? Monitoring their activities could be an organizational nightmare for a Canadian small business.

Instead we decided to use companies that were already manufacturing and selling to the U.S. paint–sundry items market and that were looking for additional products to show to buyers. In 1998 we began a relationship with a company in California that wanted to include Caulk-Rite and Caulk-Away. The company primarily sold grouting tools to home improvement retailers, including Home Depot in the U.S.

For 18 months they had exclusive rights to sell our tools in the States. We sat back and waited. They repackaged the tools for the American market, but in terms of sales nothing happened. It soon became apparent that this company, which was quite staid and old-fashioned, was contracting rather than expanding. The sales director, who we really liked, left and no caulking tools were ordered. It was time to move on.

Caulk-Rite's main competitor in the U.S. is a small, square, plastic object that was sold in Canada until we managed to show that we had a better mousetrap. This product is still sold extensively in the U.S. by one company. During our rounds of trade shows, we had met representatives of this company on a number of occasions, and they expressed interest in Vancouver Tool Corporation and our products, which were, of course, directly challenging theirs. In 2001 we signed an agreement with them to market Caulk-Rite, Caulk-Away, Caulk-Kit, and Caulk-Doctor in the U.S. This agreement is still in effect. Although sales have increased (Caulk-Rite and Caulk-Away are available at Ace stores and Caulk-Rite in Lowe's), they are extremely disappointing compared with what they have been in Canada. This is probably the result of two factors: first, the company has its own caulk applicator, which it continues to market in preference to our caulk applicator; and second, with 50 of its own products to worry about, it has other priorities.

The lesson we and every inventor or small business person eventually learns is that no one can sell or market your products like you can—you are the one with a personal commitment to the products. While our U.S. distributor has made some inroads in the American market, it has done little to help us land a contract with Home Depot, the big fish that controls 50% of the home improvement market. This fish has been netted twice but managed to swim away on both occasions.

In 1998 I learned Home Depot USA had two "open to buy" days a year. These are days when Home Depot buyers are available to meet with vendors and review new products. I had learned about this event through Industry Canada and a gentleman working at its Los Angeles office. We met with the Home Depot buyer in Seattle; he decided to list the tools, but he wanted us to ship directly to 80 stores in the western U.S. In 1999 we knew we were not ready or able to do this.

In 2001, as we were negotiating with the U.S. distributor, we attended another Home Depot "open to buy" day, in Anaheim, California. We had just completed a trade show in Germany and flown 20 hours to reach California, missed our connection to Anaheim and had to drive the final 125 miles (200 kilometres) to arrive in time for a 9 a.m. meeting. This meeting went well. The Home Depot buyer (a woman) saw the demonstration and handed us a Home Depot vendor agreement to complete. We left exhausted and elated, expecting to hand this document to our new U.S. distributor and then watch them service Home Depot, a firm they were already dealing with. Four years later our products have yet to appear in Home Depots in the U.S. Despite promises that "it will only be a matter of time" and that they have excellent relationships with "The Depot," the big fish is still not caught.

Other Canadian small businesses have told me that many American buyers have no desire to buy products from a small foreign company. Our relationship with our U.S. distributor *should* have solved this problem for us and has not. Naturally we have spoken to them about this, but we have an agreement with them and they are achieving the minimums (which we naïvely set too low in 2000), so unless the sales and performance improve, we have to wait out the agreement and then try again.

It still surprises me (and the U.S. residents who call us regularly after not finding caulking tools in their local retail outlets) that American buyers can be so resistant. It is not as if we are selling a completely untested product. Our products have satisfied countless mail-order customers in the U.S. and retail customers in Canada. All that Home Depot USA needs to do is obtain sales figures for caulking tools from its Canadian counterpart to see there is no risk. But it has not done this. The wall of the U.S. dam has started to crack, though, with Lowe's, Ace Hardware, and Menards, so we hope the flood will come soon. In two years our relationship with this distributor ends, and we will be able to make a well-researched business decision based on our experiences.

Selling to Europe

Sales to Europe have progressed haphazardly. Following our second Canadian National Hardware Show, we made contact with Vitrex, a company based in England that ordered the Caulk-Rite tool made in its own corporate colour with its logo. This was in 1998. The following year we were delighted to learn it had placed Caulk-Rite in the third-largest home improvement retailer in Britain: Wickes, with branding in the Wickes colour. The only problem was that the tool had been placed in the tiling section rather than the sealant section of the stores, so any customer looking for caulk-related products could not find it. Consequently sales were slow. (Later we lost this contract when Vitrex brought out its own tools to sell to Wickes.)

In January 2000 we took part in the Do-It-Yourself Show in London, England. This was an extremely expensive show, very male, very smoky, and very hot. While we made a number of contacts, subsequent sales were disappointing. At the time

At the Do-It-Yourself
Show in London,
England, with the
Canadian trade
minister

we did receive a lot of support, although no money, from the Canadian government. As a Canadian small business you soon learn there are few dollars available for entrepreneurs, just encouragement. The Canadian trade minister came to visit our booth and we got our photograph taken with him, but beyond this and a few free maple leaf flags, the support was disappointing. A year later I was invited to a women's trade mission to London led by the Canadian government, and there I met a number of prescreened U.K. companies that were interested in our tools. One of these companies, called Vortex, manufactured sealant in Northern England and sold to Europe and Africa. When Vortex expressed interest in an exclusive arrangement to sell VTC products, we agreed and informed Vitrex (with whom we did not have an exclusive agreement) that Vortex would be selling the product in future.

Vortex was a family-owned concern headed by a huge and hearty man in his late fifties with excellent interpersonal skills. Our relationship ended in 2003 when his company went bankrupt. During that time sales to Europe did not increase, but we did secure orders from Ceys—one of the largest sealant manufacturers in Spain. We had a really good personal relationship with Vortex, stayed at the family home and genuinely liked the company of the owner. The problem was that the owner was winding down his involvement in the business and his two sons did not have the same spark their father did. I do not hold anyone responsible in this instance. It just demonstrates the totally unpredictable nature of business.

So in late 2003 when sales of the Caulk-Doctor were booming in the U.S., we were left with little in Europe. At that time I received a call from the publisher of *Hardware Merchandising* asking if I could be persuaded to exhibit at the 2004 Cologne International Hardware Show in Germany in return for some free advertising in three magazines. We decided to take the plunge (see Appendix 4).

The four-day Cologne show takes a week out of your life. You spend two days travelling and have no time to recover from jet lag. You then spend one day on set-up and four days working the show. The cost of flights, accommodation, meals, show space, insurance, and so on added up to around $15,000. But within

Booth set-up at International Hardware Show in Cologne, Germany

six months of our return we had recouped this expenditure with initial sales to Australia, Sweden, Denmark, Belgium, Spain, Poland, and England. These sales have confirmed my belief in the marketing advantages of trade shows.

We sell only bulk (unpackaged) tools to Europe, and for the most part we sell only Caulk-Rite and Caulk-Away, in plastic and metal. We air-freight tools so customers receive them within a week of placing an order, and we price in Eurodollars. Payment is made through electronic transfers. Initial orders are always the hardest, as mountains of paper have to accompany the shipment and each country has different paperwork requirements. In addition, there is always the risk that the purchaser will not pay the bill. Although we usually ask for a minimum order of 5,000 units, we often waive this requirement for new customers who need a smaller quantity in order to kick sales into action. We use a fantastic family-owned international courier service based at Vancouver Airport and ship to our customer's nearest international airport. We pay the freight and it is the customer's responsibility to pay duties and taxes.

Being in Vancouver means Europe is eight time zones ahead, and personal conversations, even if we could speak every European language, are difficult. Most ordering and negotiating take place by fax and email. Consequently the first thing I do in the morning is respond to the emails that have arrived during the night from all over the world. Following a trade show, the number can be considerable.

One small business operator in Ontario has told me he is not interested in European sales and feels that the population of this continent is quite sufficient for his company to achieve profitable sales. The same argument could be used for VTC. Part of our desire to explore other markets comes from having European roots ourselves and from enjoying the contacts and challenges. It is great to get faxes from Australia, emails from Sweden, and phone calls from Poland (even if you do not understand every word and wonder at the end of the conversation what exactly you have agreed to). We get excited hearing that Caulk-Rite is available in a home improvement store in Belgium or seeing Caulk-Away packaged in Spanish or getting an inquiry from Italy. We may eventually decide that the uncoordinated way we have proceeded in Europe—where we have not tried to get the tools sold specifically in one region or through one distributor—has been a mistake. But in the meantime, we're having fun.

Advice for the inventor

1. If employing sales agents or manufacturers' agents, ensure they have a good knowledge of the market. If possible, obtain references and establish a formal contract with them.

2. Accept the fact that no one will work as hard as you, the inventor, to sell and market the products.

3. Expect a number of things to occur over which you have no control. Sales people move on, companies fold, buyers change, and again the cruel (or kind) hand of fate comes into play. It is the nature of business.

4. Decide which market you want to penetrate and devise a strategy for that market. The markets closest to home may not necessarily be the easiest ones to enter.

5. If signing a long-term agreement with exclusivity rights, ensure you are completely happy with it and that you agree with *all* the clauses. Be sure you can regularly monitor performance. If you can afford to, consult a lawyer.

6. If selling to Europe, give prices in Euros. If selling to the United States, give prices in U.S. dollars.

7. Whenever possible, provide pricing to the nearest international airport or seaport.

8. Be aware that packaging requirements differ from country to country and, if possible, sell your invention without packaging.

CHAPTER 8: **The Inventor's Future**

Maintain, Develop, or Sell?

We do not want to own Vancouver Tool Corporation forever. Both Andrew and I have 101 things to try while we are still able. We seek new challenges and changes. In many respects VTC inhibits our ambitions because we spend so much time and energy thinking about caulking and grouting tools that we are not at liberty to pursue other dreams. In this regard we are different from the true entrepreneur who wants to build an empire.

The pursuit of profit has never been my primary goal. The pursuit of fun has. A few years ago I attended a seminar for small businesses, and the speaker, an accountant, said that often the most successful entrepreneurs are not the ones who want to make money but the ones who genuinely enjoy what they are doing. When we tell family and friends we are thinking about what to do next, they are surprised: "How could you possibly leave your baby of a business now, when all the really hard work has been done and the future looks good?" Even the professionals we have spoken to express amazement: "Why would anyone want to leave this cash cow? Is there something you are not telling us?" But for us it is a quality-of-life issue. We are both in our mid-forties and time is marching on. We want to learn what options are available.

We have proved we can launch a new invention, we can grow a business, and we can become profitable. Goals have been achieved. After nine years we are considering what to do next. We seem to have three options:

- Maintain the status quo.
- Grow the business.
- Sell the business.

Maintain the status quo

Because everything changes on a day-to-day basis in the world of business, it is not really possible to "maintain the status quo." The nature of VTC means that we never know whether that buyer from Germany we spoke to six months ago will suddenly order 100,000 units or whether Canadian Tire will discover a better caulking tool and stop ordering ours. We can maintain the status quo by not actively seeking new business, but this is boring. The invention, production, and marketing of a new product are extremely costly, risky, and time-consuming, but at the same time these activities are exciting, stimulating, and fun. With more than 10 products available and a staff of two, VTC cannot afford to develop new items. Andrew would love to invent more but this is just not practical. Inventions need marketing, and that's the time-consuming part. The priority has to be to increase or maintain sales to existing markets, not to develop new products or explore totally new markets. The question is whether the status quo is a feasible option and whether it will keep us stimulated.

The strange irony is that while we are not brave enough to radically expand VTC, we know we will be frustrated if we continue in this current developmental state.

Grow the business

Although VTC has grown consistently, the growth has been a slow, organized, steady development that the two of us have managed to achieve working from home. There is a point, and this point has probably been reached, at which we can only increase sales and grow the business significantly if we make a number of radical changes. These changes would involve recruiting staff for administration, sales, and shipping and receiving; purchasing or leasing a warehouse (we currently store product at our packaging company); purchasing our own injection molding machinery; and acquiring office space. Significant capital expenditure would have to be found for set-up costs. I have no doubt we could do this, either through venture capital or bank loans, but this growth is daunting and the risks great. More important, we have no ambition to see VTC grow in this way.

If asked to discuss our case, the M.B.A. crew would argue that this is the way we should proceed. They would say that with a proven track record and international patents in place, we could achieve a return on investment in a relatively short time just by, for example, penetrating the U.S. market. The home improvement industry and consumer expenditure on house renovation continue to grow, the market is strong, and the risk under safe management is minimal. We know the arguments and do not doubt the experts are correct. Two less reluctant capitalists would have probably taken this path earlier. We are either too cowardly and too foolish to recognize the full potential or, as I believe, have no yearning to dedicate the rest of our lives to the sale of caulking tools. When I am on my deathbed I do not want to look back and see my contribution to society in terms of neatly caulked bathtubs. It is time to move on.

We could also easily grow the business by marketing other people's inventions. Whenever we receive media coverage we end up with a number of inquiries from inventors all over North America who want us to take their fantastic little devices onboard. Some of these calls come from inventors who only have an idea and no tangible product, others come from inventors who have produced thousands of items, which are now in storage waiting to be sold. These inventors are prepared to offer VTC a small commission for marketing services, but we always refuse these offers. With our experience of taking an invention to the marketplace, we could easily expand or launch another business just to market new inventions, but we know, as do the inventors who approach us, that inventing is relatively easy compared with selling a new idea.

Sell the business

Like all aspects of business (marketing, sales, exporting, recruiting staff, insurance, legal matters, etc.) there are seminars on selling your baby, run by a plethora of business experts. Over the last few years we have attended a few of these workshops in order to gain some insight into the process. Business gurus suggest all business owners need an "exit strategy," and that you should explore the options whether or not you are serious about selling.

The first two seminars we attended were offered by medium-sized Vancouver-based accounting/financial firms. These sessions cost approximately $100 for a three- to four-hour presentation. Both were quite informative. Suited men told us about the mathematical calculations used to value a business, be it a coffee shop, auto repair shop, or private school. In looking at these samples (and focusing primarily on historical sales trends), we saw how established businesses trading in recognized commercial sectors could be valued.

These financial wizards spoke about finding a "fair market value" for your business: a cash sum agreed upon by two parties who had discussed all the facts. They also enlightened us about "strategic buyers" who might acquire a business with specific side benefits in mind. For example, a manufacturer wanting to sell to Canadian Tire might purchase VTC if he saw it as an easy way to access this retailer, or a sealant manufacturer might purchase VTC in order to use our tools to facilitate sales of sealant. Combining two existing businesses creates certain advantages. A strategic buyer will pay more for a business than will a "financial buyer" who is only interested in the fair market price.

We found it difficult to think about setting a price for VTC, which is a relatively new business with unique intellectual property (how do you value a patent?) and with potential for growth that few can predict. In a number of informal chats with experts, the phrase "you'll get what the market will bear" kept coming up. So what would the market bear? The experts would not speculate and instead just questioned why we even wanted to get out when VTC was at a significant growth stage.

Early in 2003 we attended a two-day seminar on selling a business as part of our plan to test the waters and find out about the value of VTC. The presentation took place at a five-star hotel in downtown Vancouver and was given by a large California-based company with offices in Toronto. About 20 Canadian companies were attending. Social interaction proved to be a little strained, as few people wanted to say exactly what their companies did or who they were. The seminar commenced with the charismatic speaker asking us to put pen to paper and calculate the value of a hypothetical business. We all obediently followed his every step. After 20 minutes he told us to tear up our calculations because "a business is worth whatever the market will bear."

After the seminar, we spent almost $50,000 on a contract with this company to market and perhaps sell VTC over the next five years. In addition to the initial large sum for evaluation, we agreed to pay a commission if a sale was achieved. For the next four months this company worked at producing a fantastic 50-page confidential business review detailing every aspect of VTC and another 50-page evaluation report that basically provided background on the home improvement industry. We supplied the numbers and the firm's staff did the analyses and wrote the reports.

One of the disadvantages of running your own business is that you can never take the time to step back and evaluate the business. This company managed to do that for us and succeeded in offering a detached yet informative in-depth review. They gave us a range of figures for the offers they believed we would receive and told us how they planned to market the business. Although $50,000 may seem like a lot of money, we feel we received good value for this expenditure. The firm provided us with an honest and detailed analysis of VTC and, more importantly, explained the process of selling a business.

Once the confidential business report was complete, including all the financial statements and projections, our broker created a one-page summary about VTC. He then identified more than 1,500 prospective buyers around the world and sent them the summary and a letter. This resulted in 40 requests for additional information. The broker sent the full report to these interested parties and talked to them by telephone before receiving five serious expressions of interest.

During this time the broker, a somewhat solemn man from Seattle with a deep love of dining out in Vancouver, came to see us on a number of occasions for either lunch or dinner. During these two- to four-hour meetings we learned a lot about selling a business, not just our own. He explained that one of the biggest problems we faced was in being home-based. While our sales figures were good, many of the bigger players would not take us seriously.

But there was yet another problem. The contract with our U.S. distributor stated that it had the right to match any offer placed by any potential buyer. This contract also gave it the exclusive rights to distribute the products in the United States until September 2006. Once other potential buyers learned of this, they declined to make an offer. What was the point when it could just be matched? In 2004 our U.S. distributor did place an offer, which we rejected. Just after we received and rejected the offer, our broker's contract was terminated. It seemed the right time to put everything on hold, to regroup and consider what to do next.

The 18-month selling process clearly taught us three things:

- Our U.S. distributor places little value on our business. (Our suspicions about unenthusiastic marketing of our tools in the U.S. were seemingly confirmed.)
- Selling a business takes time, and perhaps we need to take our business to the next stage of development in order to attract a significantly better offer. (This next stage involves concentrating on sales to the United States.)
- Selling a business does not necessarily mean the original owner no longer has a role to play. (Many prospective buyers expected us to stay with VTC until the hand-over took place to ensure that sales continued to grow.)

In my naïveté I had believed that selling a business was like selling a car or a house: you agree to a price and then on a certain date a change of ownership occurs. The more I learn about the process, the more I realize it is not like this. Buyers frequently stipulate your involvement for a specified period of time—usually two or three years. An agreed-upon sum is paid once the ownership changes, and another sum is paid at a later date. This second sum is usually dependent on the maintenance or growth of sales. These arrangements can mean that the original owner's departure from the business is a long and drawn-out affair that requires working with the new owner.

The whole process of exploring what to do next has taught us that it is never too early to consider an exit strategy. Even if you are unsure whether you want to sell your business, the learning process is fascinating. Just going through the selling process was a positive experience for us. It confirmed that what we are doing is precisely what we should be doing. This lesson, and the positive reinforcement we received from the independent advisors, has managed to inject a renewed vigour, enthusiasm, and interest into our approach to the business.

I sincerely hope we do *not* own VTC in 20 years, even if it is 100 times more profitable than it is today. At the same time, we are not quite ready to forsake VTC after all the effort we have put into growing and nurturing our baby. Not one financial advisor has advised us to sell. Perhaps we should learn to take the advice of these experts on this matter.

Licensing agreements

One further option is available to the inventor who has patents. It involves issuing a licensing agreement that allows a manufacturer to produce and sell the patented item. The manufacturer then pays a royalty to the patent holder for each product sold.

We have considered and rejected this option because we believe such agreements would be difficult to monitor and would lead to organizational headaches. For the established inventor with existing market penetration, there is little advantage. I suspect, though, that for the inventor with a new product and no capital or marketing expertise, the royalty route could be attractive. However, I have to say that in 20 years of being around inventors I do not know of one who has successfully managed to secure a licensing agreement. A Holy Grail, perhaps?

Conclusion?

There is no conclusion. I would love to write that we have just signed an agreement to sell Vancouver Tool Corporation for X million dollars and that following a six-month trip around the world I will be starting flying lessons and Andrew will be designing our new house ... but this is not the case. The inventor's story is unfinished, but there is still a happy ending. We have taken a new invention from the mind to the marketplace, we have made money, and we are having fun. While the future is somewhat uncertain, I have no regrets about being Canada's largest manufacturer of caulking tools.

Advice for the inventor

1. It is never too soon to consider an "exit strategy," although serious offers will probably not be forthcoming until patents and orders are in place.

2. Attend business seminars on buying and selling a business to learn as much as possible.

3. If you are serious about selling, consider hiring a professional organization with expertise in this area to undertake an in-depth analysis of every aspect of your business. If nothing else you will end up with an unbiased evaluation of your business, including all its strengths and weaknesses, which you can then use to decide whether to maintain, grow, or sell your business.

4. If you decide to sell your business, do not try to market it yourself. Doing so takes you away from the day-to-day operation and administration of the business and could affect sales. Continue operating the business and employ other professionals to market and sell it.

5. Expect the sale of your business to take a considerable length of time.

6. If starting off in business, consider licensing your products and collecting royalties based on sales. Seek legal advice before signing any agreement.

Name/Address/ Email/Phone	Information Sent/ Samples	Follow-up/ Result
RONA		
Home Hardware		
Canadian Tire		
Home Depot		
DH Howden		
Canadian Superstore		
Wal-Mart		
Sears		

Example A

Dear _____:

Further to our brief telephone conversation earlier today, I have pleasure in sending you samples and information about our unique range of patented caulking tools.

Eight years ago The Vancouver Tool Corporation invented and started to market two unique tools for the application and removal of sealant. Unlike many other tools available, the Caulk-Rite (sealant application tool) and Caulk-Away (sealant removal tool) actually work. Buyers in North America recognized the tools' attributes. Now these tools are available in every major Canadian DIY retailer, including: Home Depot, Canadian Tire, Home Hardware, RONA, Sears, and Wal-Mart. In the United States our products are sold through distribution channels and are available in Ace Hardware Stores, Lowe's, and Menards. For your information I am sending a recent Home Depot flyer together with photographs of our products in Home Depot.

I enclose samples of our Caulk-Rite and Caulk-Away products as they are sold in North America. We have found our products sell very well when clip-stripped by the sealants and are an easy "add-on" when someone is purchasing a tube of sealant. The attached Product Information Sheet details the costs and packaging specifications.

Please visit our web site (www.vancouvertool.com) to view our full product range. Early next year we will be exhibiting at the DIY and Garden Show in London, booth number J18, where we will be demonstrating our tools. I would welcome the opportunity to meet you at this time. To enable you to try Caulk-Rite and Caulk-Away today (at your desk), I enclose two T-bars and one of our Caulk-Doctor kits (over 200,000 Caulk-Doctor Kits have been sold on the QVC shopping network in the United States; see the disk, which shows one of our many TV appearances). The Caulk-Doctor contains everything you need to try the tools.

I will telephone you in a couple of weeks to gain your reaction to these products and to answer any questions you may have. In the interim, if you require more samples of these or of any of our other products, please do not hesitate to contact me (email jayne@vancouvertool.com).

I look forward to speaking with you.

Best wishes,

Jayne Seagrave
Marketing Director

Example B

Dear _____:

Thank you for your fax requesting samples of the Caulk-Kit.

I have supplied 5 samples of the packaged Caulk-Kit, carded with English, French, and Spanish instructions, and 5 samples of the unpackaged kits. If your customers are in Italy you may wish to go with the unpackaged version, as this is considerably cheaper because we would not be shipping a lot of air.

The price of the Caulk-Kit packaged in Euros = _____

The price of the Caulk-Kit unpackaged but supplied in a plastic bag in Euros = _____

Prices include shipping to your nearest international airport. Minimum order 2,000 units.

I am sorry we do not have a catalogue, but we can supply a disk with our graphics should you wish to make one yourself. We do have the enclosed English-only leaflets.

I hope I have supplied all the information you require. Please do not hesitate to contact me again should you require anything else.

Best wishes,

Jayne Seagrave
Marketing Director

Example A

PRODUCT INFORMATION SHEET:
CAULK-RITE-PRO

Description:
Hand-held, 10" steel, patented tool with rubber-bladed end for the application and finishing of silicone and caulk.

Price:

Recommended Retail:
US$9.99 – US$11.99

Freight: FOB Vancouver, Canada.

Packaging:
Heavy-Duty Clam-Shell Blister:
   13" by 3.5". Depth = 2.5". Weight = 0.25 lb.
Inner Pack = 9" by 3.5" by 13". Quantity = 5. Weight = 1.5 lb.
Master Pack = 18" by 15" by 13". Quantity = 25. Weight = 7.25 lb.

Lead Time/Terms:
2-4 weeks
30 days – 2%

Origin:
Canadian produced and manufactured

UPC Code:
6 24939 00010 8

Sales and Marketing Contact:
Jayne Seagrave

Example B

PRODUCT INFORMATION SHEET:
CAULK-AWAY-PRO

Description:
Hand-held, 10" steel, patented tool with metal-bladed end for the removal of silicone and caulk.

Price:

Recommended Retail:
US$9.99 – US$11.99

Freight: FOB Vancouver, Canada.

Packaging:
Heavy-Duty Clam-Shell Blister:
   13" by 3.5". Depth = 2.5" Weight = 0.25 lb.
Inner Pack = 9" by 3.5" by 13". Quantity = 5. Weight = 1.5 lb.
Master Pack = 18" by 15" by 13". Quantity = 25. Weight = 7.25 lb.

Lead Time/Terms:
2-4 weeks.
30 days – 2%

Origin:
Canadian produced and manufactured

UPC Code:
6 24939 00011 5

Sales and Marketing Contact:
Jayne Seagrave

Example C

PRODUCT INFORMATION SHEET:
CAULK-RITE-PRO

Canadian Patent #2158873. U.S. Patent #6219878.
European Patent #853711.

Important Information:
Unique, patented product.
The only professional tool for the application of caulk.
Competitively priced.
Allows the creation of the perfect caulking bead.
No mess or edge marks.
Conforms to any angle.
No wasted caulk.
Suitable for any caulk application.
Replacement blades available.

Product Description:
The new, unique, heavy-duty Caulk-Rite-Pro with its revolutionary design helps beginner and expert create the perfect caulking bead every time. Formed in heavy-duty steel, it is the professional way to apply caulk and an answer to the contractor's nightmares.

Information for Buyers:
The red plastic Caulk-Rite tool is the most versatile caulk-application tool on the market, sold by every major home improvement retailer in Canada and available in Lowe's and Ace stores in the USA and an easy add-on for the customer of caulking. The new Caulk-Rite-Pro has been developed for the professional/contractor for the application of caulk and sealants in a consistent, perfect manner. The heavy-duty clam-shell blister protects the tool, and the packaging is trilingual (English, French, and Spanish) with illustrations. The packaging has been designed to illustrate every aspect of the tool and can be easily clip-stripped with professional tools, tiling accessories, bathroom accessories, and sealants. Replacement blades available.

Competitive Information:
No other caulk-application tool can create different sizes of caulk bead, nor do competitors' tools work on differing angles. This is the only caulk-application tool available specifically for the professional renovator and contractor.

Example D

PRODUCT INFORMATION SHEET:
CAULK-AWAY-PRO

Canadian Patent #2219468. U.S. Patent #6035536.
European Patent # 924366.

Important Information:
Unique, patented product.
The only professional tool for the removal of caulk.
Competitively priced.
No chemicals required.
Can be sharpened for reuse.
Multiple cutting points and scraping edges.
Suitable for any caulk removal.
Replacement blades available.

Product Description:
The new, unique, heavy-duty Caulk-Away-Pro with its revolutionary design helps beginner and expert easily remove caulk and silicon. The body is formed in heavy-duty steel while the blade is made from hard stainless spring steel. It is the professional way to remove caulk and an answer to the contractor's problems.

Information for Buyers:
The red plastic Caulk-Away tool is the most versatile caulk-removal tool on the market, sold by every major home improvement retailer in Canada and an easy add-on for the customer of caulking. The new Caulk-Away-Pro has been developed for the professional/contractor for the removal of caulk and sealants in a consistent, perfect manner. The heavy-duty clam-shell blister protects the tool, and the packaging is trilingual (English, French, and Spanish) with illustrations. The packaging has been designed to illustrate every aspect of the tool and can be easily clip-stripped with professional tools, tiling accessories, bathroom accessories, and sealants. Replacement blades available.

Competitive Information:
No other caulk-removal tool has been designed with so many cutting and scraping edges and a rear point for removing caulk in multiple situations. The Caulk-Away-Pro tool provides the perfect alternative to screwdrivers or chemical removers.

Example A

PRESS RELEASE
Caulking the Professional Way

At last, two tools have been developed to assist the professional contractor to apply and remove caulk: Caulk-Rite-Pro and Caulk-Away-Pro. Following the success of the smaller plastic tools, Caulk-Rite and Caulk-Away, these new items made in heavy-duty steel come with replacement blades and have been designed by the Vancouver Tool Corporation specifically with the professional in mind.

Says president of the Vancouver Tool Corporation Andrew Dewberry: "In my previous life as an architect I witnessed hundreds of contractors on site using blunt chisels to remove caulk and then reapplying it with their fingers. There are much better uses to put your fingers to, so I invented tools to ensure the neat and easy removal and application of caulk."

Caulk-Rite-Pro is a patented, 10-inch, hand-held, heavy-duty metal tool with a rubber end that creates the perfect caulking bead every time. Replacement blades are also available. Likewise Caulk-Away-Pro has an extremely sharp blade with multiple cutting edges, is made from stainless spring steel with a 10-inch handle formed from strong metal and is the only caulk-removal tool designed specifically with the professional in mind. Both tools retail for under $20 each and are packaged in a clam-shell blister with trilingual instructions. See both tools at the International Hardware Fair, Cologne, Germany, 14-17 March 2004, Hall 10, Aisle E, Booth No. 044.

-30-

For more information, contact:
Jayne Seagrave
Tel: Fax:
Or visit our web site: www.vancouvertool.com

Example B

PRESS RELEASE
Free Tools at Totally Tools!

The Vancouver Tool Corporation (VTC), Canada's largest manufacturer of sealant and grouting tools, will be giving away over 200 of its unique, patented Seal-Rite sealant-application tools at the DIY and Garden/Totally Tools Show to the first 200 visitors to its stand, located at J18.

Says Marketing Director Jayne Seagrave: "Our sealant tools are sold in all the major DIY chains in North America, including Home Depot, Wal-Mart, Lowe's, RONA, and Canadian Tire. We are exhibiting at the DIY Show as we believe it to be excellent opportunity to showcase the products in Europe. We will be demonstrating the products at our stand, as this is the best way to show the unique attributes of our sealant tools and ensure that we get the products out there. 200 Seal-Rite tools will be given away."

The Vancouver Tool Corporation produces tools for both the professional and do-it-yourself markets. Each year over one million of its sealant tools are sold in North America alone. For those not so interested in sealant tools, Canadian maple butter cookies will also be on offer, courtesy of VTC. So if you are hungry for new products—or just hungry—visit Vancouver Tool at stand J18.

-30-

For more information or a personal interview contact:
Jayne Seagrave
Tel: Fax:
Or visit our web site: www.vancouvertool.com

Example C

PRESS RELEASE

Canadians in a practical world

The phone call came early one cold Friday morning in February: "Jayne, how would you like to take part in the largest hardware show in the world, in Cologne, Germany, next month? We need more Canadian companies to take part, and if you agree, I'll throw in some editorial on your new products." The timing was right. We had just severed our relationship with our European distributor (little performance), and while sales of our caulking and grouting tools were increasing in North America, this was not the case in Europe. So my response to this invitation from the publisher of *Hardware Merchandising* (one of Canada's oldest trade magazines, in which advertising for our new professional range of tools would be well placed) was "yes."

Taking part in the four-day Practical World International Hardware and Do-It-Yourself Fair is not cheap. Flights for two of us from Vancouver to Cologne, hotel rooms for six days, food, transport, show-space rental, furniture, insurance, advertising literature, shipping, etc., cost us around $15,000. In order to fund this, we decided to access Industry Canada's Program for Export Market Development (PEMD). I called my contact in the Vancouver office, who knows our company well, to ask if we were eligible. PEMD encourages companies to showcase their products in areas of the world where they have no sales. Industry Canada provides up to 50% of the expenses (to a limit of $8,000), which is repayable once sales in the target country are obtained. While our target country was Germany, we returned with sales leads from all over the globe, including Australia, New Zealand, South Africa, Italy, Hungary, Greece, Poland—even Iceland. In addition, we personally met representatives from companies in Sweden and Spain who already purchase our products, thereby facilitating that all-too-vital personal contact.

Practical World is huge. It takes place in 14 exhibition halls with over 3,500 exhibitors. In 2004 we were one of only five Canadian companies taking part. Before leaving for Cologne, I asked Industry Canada for promotional items—badges, maple-leaf stickers, flags, anything to make our Canadian exhibition stand different and to facilitate exports. I was informed that because we weren't a not-for-profit agency, these items were not available to us. I called my friend and complained. Surely for a company trying to gain export sales and, ultimately, revenue for the country, he could provide the odd flag. He did, and I demonstrated my caulking tools with red maple-leaf tattoos adorning my hands during the show.

Unlike many other trade shows, which are suffering from falling attendance numbers in North America, Practical World was busy. After the first night, we were invited to the Canada Night reception at a bar near the exhibition grounds. It was organized by "Hardlines," an internet news agency based in Toronto that specializes in news about the hardware industry. The evening was informal and relaxed, and the international guests outnumbered the Canadians by at least two to one. Our host from Hardlines told us that for the first time, the number of Canadians at the show exceeded the number of visitors from Luxembourg; we all cheered. He spoke briefly, thanking us for coming to the Canadian party, then produced a mouth organ and played "O Canada." The six of us who knew the words sang; I had tears in my eyes. Afterwards we mingled. It was the easiest way ever to meet Canadian Tire buyers, who in our industry are true gods with purse strings.

The American reception was held the following night in a conference ballroom—no small German bar or mouth organs here. Instead, a large video screen displayed a stage performance by the singing and dancing Blues Brothers. Waiters in dinner jackets delivered a huge buffet, with free wine and beer and complimentary German beer glasses for guests to take home. The dessert menu featured 25 different delights (the dessert at the Canadian reception consisted of profiteroles, which in the dark light of the bar looked like boiled potatoes, so remained untouched). I spent three hours at this reception talking to people from Germany, Japan, Sweden, Holland, and England. Only in the last few minutes did we actually converse with one of the hosts.

The Practical World fair was an exhausting four days, each one lasting from 9 a.m. until 6 p.m. We were in the international section, where four out of the five exhibiting Canadian companies were located. This section generated a considerable amount of traffic, with international buyers looking for items already proven in markets in other parts of the world. We collected over 150 business cards from individuals who were interested in our tools. At the end of each day I divided these into three categories as follows: "No action"—filed away but kept, because someone could contact us again and it's always good to see the card; "thanks"—these are contacts who receive a "thanks for calling by our booth" letter reminding them they were interested in our products (but after this correspondence, no further action is taken); and finally, "hot leads"—this is the most labour-intensive but potentially rewarding group.

We will not know whether Practical World has been profitable for our business for quite a while, until the orders come in. Personally I had a wonderful time, but that could be because I really like German beer. I do find it sad that more Canadian hardware companies didn't make the effort to take part, and even more alarming that Industry Canada did not have a presence. Hopefully in 2006, when the fair is held again, Canadians will continue to outnumber visitors from Luxembourg and the Canadian party will be just as much fun.

-30-

For more information or a personal interview contact:
Jayne Seagrave
Tel: Fax:
Or visit our web site: www.vancouvertool.com

(Note: Press releases should be double-spaced and end with "-30-", centred on the page after the last line.)

Trade Shows Attended by VTC 1996–2005

Name	Location	Date
Western Hardware Show	Vancouver, Canada	October 1996
Smith Barrager Dealer Show	Vancouver, Canada	February 1997
Canadian National Hardware Show	Toronto, Canada	February 1997
Paint and Decorating Show	Los Angeles, USA	March 1997
Home Hardware Dealers' Market	St. Jacobs, Canada	April 1997
Federated Coops Spring Market	Saskatoon, Canada	May 1997
Home Hardware Dealers' Market	St. Jacobs, Canada	September 1997
Paint and Decorating Show Paint Show	St. Louis, USA Portland, USA	October 1997 November 1997
Canadian National Hardware Show	Toronto, Canada	February 1998
Home Hardware Dealers' Market	St. Jacobs, Canada	April 1998
Pro Show Sherwin Williams	Seattle, USA	April 1998

Kitchen and Bath Show	Chicago, USA	April 1998
Atlantic Builders' Show	Moncton, Canada	April 1998
Home Hardware Dealers' Market	St. Jacobs, Canada	September 1998
DH Howden Dealers' Market	Mississauga, Canada	October 1998
American Hardware Show	Chicago, USA	August 1999
Do-It-Yourself Trade Show	London, England	January 2000
Canadian National Hardware Show	Toronto, Canada	February 2000
Cologne International Hardware Fair	Cologne, Germany	March 2001
American Hardware Show	Chicago, USA	August 2001
Cologne International Hardware Fair	Cologne, Germany	March 2004
Western Supply Building Dealers' Show	Abbotsford, Canada	January 2005
DIY and Garden Show	London, England	January 2005
Home Hardware Dealers' Market	St. Jacobs, Canada	April 2005

By the Same Author

Introduction to Policing in Canada (Prentice Hall)

Jayne Seagrave's Camping British Columbia: A Complete Guide to Provincial and National Park Campgrounds (Heritage House)

British Columbia's Best Camping Adventures: Southwestern BC and Vancouver Island (Heritage House)

British Columbia's Best Camping Adventures: Northern, Central, and Southeastern BC (Heritage House)

Camping with Kids: The Best Family Campgrounds in British Columbia and Alberta (Heritage House)